MINDCHANGE

'The difficulty with Leadership is that it is like the proverbial elephant: difficult to describe when it is absent, entirely obvious when it is present. For most of history we have been content to recognise it in our best leaders but not to worry too much how they came to have it. It is unlikely that Alexander the Great or Ethelred the Unready read self help books.

Today we see leadership as a utilitarian skill rather than something sent to us by the Gods or effortlessly imbibed at public school or Sandhurst. We have learned to our cost that human beings want to be led and are surprisingly uncritical of their leaders – even when they are so clearly taking them to Armageddon. We need a science of leadership if we are to avoid its pitfalls.

'Mindchange' is therefore an important contribution to the debate on how leadership works and how we ought to bend it to our moral purpose. By concentrating on equipping ourselves with emotional intelligence, we are provided with a finger post to moral leadership. We are also equipped to be more effective in gaining the following of others and the fulfilment of goals. We deploy principles to resist unethical behaviour and stand for the rights of others when it might be easier to see them as necessary victims of progress. You will still need to be driven, as only true leaders are driven, but by following 'Mindchange's' r   will make it much more likely that you will succeed and that you   nd.'

Lord Poole

t in leadership

'In a wide ranging review of ....   rly management gurus to recent Gallup work in customer trust and events including Enron, Worldcom, Iraq and the Tsunami, and even the current yoof culture of Hip-Hop, Jan and David have eloquently explored the relevance and importance of EQ and its linkage with authentic leadership.

At times I found the alternation between a précis of thinking across the eras,

the guidance on EQ4U, their simple but effective process for developing EQ, and the analysis of recent case studies disrupting, but in retrospect I found this integrative approach effective in giving me a holistic understanding of EQ, the case for it and practical guidance on developing it in myself.

All in all, an important and useful read for any leader (which should be every leader) with ambitions to inspire followers – the test of leadership being an ability to create willing followers!'

Bob Bradley, Regional Chairman
The Academy for Chief Executives

'Leadership is an enormous subject with a bewildering array of books on it. If one is to learn more about improving leadership skills, where should you start? 'Mindchange' addresses that area of leadership now defined as Emotional Intelligence and provides a practical tool with which to start your own development. The book sets out the development of Emotional Intelligence with quick reviews of previous work and explains the needs behind the approach. Our world now is an uncertain place filled with conflicting elements. Those elements often seem to erupt into violence; the resolution of which is neither easy nor clear cut. The ambiguous nature of the conflicts and their roots gives all those who would aspire to a leadership position a huge challenge. 'Mindchange' reminds us all that it is people that cause conflicts and it is people that will resolve them; only by understanding yourself and others, and listening and responding to them in an ethical manner – EQ4U – will we be able to move forward.'

John Jupp

'Mindchange' addresses one of the enduring challenges of exceptional leadership: how to unlock greater human capacity for achievement by developing emotional intelligence, not just intellect. This valuable book by Childs and Pardey presents new insights and practical strategies aimed at helping leaders succeed in a changing world.'

Robert K Cooper, Ph.D.
Chair, Advanced Excellence Systems LLC
Co-Author of *Executive EQ* and author of *The Other 90%*

MINDCHANGE
The power of emotionally intelligent leadership

Jan Childs and David Pardey

2000

658 . 4092

For a complete list of Management Books 2000 titles,
visit our web-site on http://www.mb2000.com

First published in 2005 by Management Books 2000 Ltd
Forge House, Limes Road
Kemble, Cirencester
Gloucestershire, GL7 6AD, UK
Tel: 0044 (0) 1285 771441
Fax: 0044 (0) 1285 771055
E-mail: info@mb2000.com
Web: www.mb2000.com

Printed and bound in Great Britain by Digital Books Logistics Ltd of Peterborough

British Library Cataloguing in Publication Data is available

ISBN 1-85252-484-7

Contents

Contents

Acknowledgements

To our clients and interviewees for providing the opportunity to discuss and share learning about their valued experience in delivering emotionally intelligent leadership. To our friends and associates for their interest, feedback and support, with special thanks to Andy, Sarah, Diana and Julius. To Liz, for all the coffee and encouragement; to James our publisher, for his enthusiasm, suggestions and shared commitment. Finally a special thank you to Ian Leath, who not only shared his first hand experience with us for the 'Latin America Dilemma' case study, but also proposed **MINDCHANGE** as the name for our book title and was a continuing source of inspiration and support.

For Jamie, Tom and Sam

Opening Reflections

MINDCHANGE is about challenging leaders at every level to develop and maintain a mindset based on continually being open to learn and change both at a personal and interpersonal level, within a framework of fundamental principles, values and applied integrity. Central to this approach is an acknowledgement of our own and others' emotions and the part these play in influencing attitude and behaviour.

We all know that cruel physical behaviour from the extremes of torture through to varying levels of physical abuse incite emotions such as anger, fear, resentment, dislike and hatred. But psychological mistreatment such as bullying, discrimination, put-downs or any situation where lack of respect is demonstrated, also provokes negative emotions that are often similar to and sometimes more intense than being subjected to physical abuse. For instance, psychological continual bullying can lead to a lack of self-esteem that can in turn lead to depression, self harm and even suicide. While the perpetrator/s may not acknowledge its impact or put this on a par with physical abuse, a range of similar emotions can be felt by their victims.

These may seem dramatic statements, but most of us only need to reflect on situations when our opinion was ignored, we were subjected to 'put downs' or in any way felt we had not been treated with respect to recognise the emotional impact of such behaviour. Just the *perception* of psychological abuse or lack of respect (whether this is intended or not) can also have a similar impact.

So, what's this got to do with leadership? Research by Surcon International (2004) suggests that up to 50% of an organisation's productivity is predictable based on employees' feelings and opinions. According to surveys, up to 85% of people believe they could double their productivity ... *'If I wanted to'* ... and they don't want to.

Why?

Lack of effective leadership is the key reason cited for lack of motivation and its consequent impact on productivity. Whatever the size and complexity of the organisation, the quality of leadership and its leaders' ability to inspire others is fundamental to maximising productivity and thus increasing profits.

We therefore believe that the power and ability of leaders at every level and within every type of organisation, both individually and collectively to influence others by *'emotional engagement'* is as important as their intellectual contributions. Whether this is leadership in business, in politics or in the community, creating an achievement culture through productive working relationships based on mutual trust has benefits that go far beyond involvement with the people directly concerned.

It is increasingly apparent that there is a convincing 'hard case for soft skills' and that the (conscious or unconscious) application of integrity-based emotionally intelligent thinking and its integration into leadership decision-making is a critical component of effective performance. Emotional competence (applied EQ) can therefore achieve not only personal benefits for the people concerned but also commercial profit and political credibility. Our intention in **MINDCHANGE** is to challenge leadership practice that puts expediency and short term *'quick wins'* before integrity, ethics and the development of valued and long-term business and personal relationships. Our aim is to stimulate and inspire a leadership approach at all levels and in all organisations that puts emotional intelligence at the forefront of decision-making and to express our passionate belief in the value of EQ and its application.

We also believe that increasing global interdependence and the danger of becoming *'anaesthetised'* to what is going on within a wider context is an issue that leaders ignore at their peril, in particular, by becoming immune to the emotions felt by those who suffer through unjust or cruel treatment and the impact this can have way beyond their immediate environment. Whether we collectively or individually have the courage or not to deal with these or ignore them;

or if the issue becomes one of fear being greater than integrity, is a matter of concern to us all.

'Reflections Explored' forms the main body of **MINDCHANGE**. Part 1 examines why emotions are important, outlines the origins of the concept of emotional intelligence and introduces the **EQ4U** process model. Part 2 reflects on the leadership dimension, why EQ matters to organisations and the importance of trust. The relationship between creativity, innovation and EQ, the leadership versus management debate, the nature of strategic and operational leadership roles and the various levels of management are also explored. Part 3 reflects on the impact of EQ on culture and productivity through a selection of case studies in a variety of organisational contexts, with leadership behaviour mapped against the **EQ4U PROCESS MODEL**. Part 4 focuses on the practice of EQ leadership and the development of emotional competence. This is followed by our 'Closing Reflections', with an emphasis on the need for integrity to be at the centre of emotionally intelligent leadership for the 21st century.

We conclude **MINDCHANGE** with our own personal list of learning resources, some that are referred to in the text and others that have influenced us in some way. If you want to follow up any of the ideas in **MINDCHANGE** you may find these useful. We would very much appreciate your thoughts on the subject and welcome any feedback you are kind enough to give us.

Jan Childs & David Pardey

Contact details:

jan.childs@mdplimited.co.uk / T: +44 (0) 1453 872211
david@teamsthatwork.co.uk / T: +44 (0) 1749 673757

Reflections Explored
Part 1:
The Emotional Dimension

Emotions Are Important

*'For star performance in all jobs in every field, emotional
competence is twice as important as purely cognitive abilities.
For success at the highest levels, in leadership positions,
emotional competence accounts for virtually the entire
advantage'.*

Daniel Goleman
'Working with Emotional Intelligence' (1998)

We all know how important emotions are at key moments in our lives,
such as the birth of a much wanted child or the death of a loved one.
Nearly all human beings will have experienced the heights of
happiness and the depths of despair – very few people are so
emotionally detached that they don't experience intense emotions
such as these at some time in their lives. The strongest emotional
reactions, like the birth of our own child or the death of a parent, come
from something we have experienced ourselves. We can also
experience emotional reactions as a result of empathising with the
emotions of others. We listen to the stories that others tell us and
(most of us) can sense and understand the emotions they are
experiencing as they tell us, so that we can understand them as well.

In 2004, we saw a picture of a woman confronting soldiers in
Uganda. It was just a picture, yet it conveyed so much. The woman's
face communicated her emotions so clearly – emotions of fear,
desperation, pleading. These emotions tumbled over themselves in
the woman's attempts to save herself and others from the threat they
faced. From this one image it was possible to build up the story that
lay behind it. The tsunami on Boxing Day 2004 had the same impact.
The abiding images that the world remembers are of the destruction it
caused to property and the unprecedented cost in human lives. Images

of bewildered children who had lost their whole family and of mothers and fathers carrying the bodies of their dead children all spoke volumes about the impact that a natural disaster could have on people.

Have you ever reacted similarly to a picture or image? What were your feelings? Most people feel a sense of helplessness when they see events they can do nothing about, seeing someone so in need of help which clearly they are unable to supply. This is the effect that emotions have on us. We use other people's emotional reactions to do more than understand their feelings; we are also able to build up a sense of what has caused them and why someone is reacting as they are. Emotions aren't simply the effect of the situation in which people find themselves; there is an interaction with those events. Other people respond to how we react emotionally as well as to our actions, and that changes our world.

Traditionally, emotional reactions were something to be hidden. Revealing emotions has typically been perceived as a shortcoming, especially if this was being done by leaders or by anyone who wanted to achieve a position of power. However much they may have concerns, grief or delight in private, leaders have generally been expected to disguise these emotions in public. For too long, emotions have been seen as signs of weakness, particularly amongst men (who tend in general to monopolise leadership positions). In fact, a man who showed his emotions rather than maintaining the traditional 'stiff upper lip' was often perceived as weak and thus condemned from achieving any position of power!

Unfortunately, a culture that encourages people to hide emotions creates an environment in which not just the outward sign of emotions gets suppressed, but the emotions themselves become repressed – not showing emotions is a short step from not feeling them either.

So what are emotions for?

Emotions exist for a reason. As human beings, regardless of race, gender, status or religious beliefs, we experience emotions as part of our body's natural signalling system. Their purpose is to get us to act, whether that's fight or flight, to be happy or sad, to offer compassion and empathy or anger and discipline. They are a natural reaction to external events, part of our ability to make sense of the world around us, not just at a conscious, rational, analytical level, but at a deeper, affective level. They don't exist by chance; these emotional reactions are the result of millions of years of evolution for a reason. For example, work done at the University of Wisconsin's Laboratory for Affective Neuroscience has shown that women respond both physiologically and psychologically quite differently to their own children compared to other children. A movie showing data from a functional magnetic resonance imaging (fMRI) brain scan illustrates this quite clearly. The movie can be downloaded from their website:

http://www.news.wisc.edu/packages/emotion/media.html

This shows that one area of the brain activates when mothers see their own infants; another area activates when they see someone else's child.

Why is this? At the most basic level, emotions help us to survive in a hostile world, enabling us to react to threats faster than we would by relying solely on conscious reasoning. A mother reacts differently to her own child and is able to respond more quickly to any threat to its well-being. That's how the human species has managed to survive. Fear generates the adrenalin we need for faster flight; love is the basis for the bonds that enable children to be cared for and protected in their vulnerable years; friendship creates the willingness to risk our own safety for others and for the greater benefit of the group; and sadness is our reaction to learning about the injury to or death of those we love.

MINDCHANGE is all about emotional intelligence and its importance for effective leadership. It is also about developing and improving your emotional intelligence. It may be that our ability to empathise (and to systemise) is largely hard-wired; but, as Simon Baron-Cohen suggests (see Learning Resources), that's no reason not to maximise the abilities we've got. Furthermore, there is ample evidence to show that we can improve our intelligence in many areas through exercising our intellectual skills. If that's the case, why can't we improve our affective skills, i.e. those that relate to moods, feelings and attitudes, including our ability to recognise other people's emotions and to respond appropriately to them, as part of our development of our emotional intelligence?

But, before looking at emotional intelligence, we need to understand just what it is we mean by 'emotions'. Plenty of people talk about emotional intelligence as if it's a clearly defined concept, without even considering what we actually mean by the term. So let's look a little more closely at that curious phenomenon called emotion that affects us all.

From *acceptance* to *terror*

Emotions are those states of mind that result from external or internal stimuli. They're how we react to the world around us. Robert Gordon (writing in *The Cambridge Dictionary of Philosophy*) says that emotions can be thought of as arising from events or circumstances that 'act upon us'. This doesn't mean in a passive way, but in the sense that we are reacting to something external to us – as the *Encyclopaedia Britannica* describes them, emotions are 'the synthesis of subjective experience, expressive behaviour, and neurochemical activity'.

In other words, emotions are:

- what we experience (subjective experience) in the world about us, which is not necessarily how others experience those same events

- how we respond to that world (expressive behaviour), which in turn changes the environment through our effect on it; and

- our body's own response (neurochemical activity), which is largely outside our direct control.

17

The adrenalin rush caused by fear and the muscle spasms that create a genuine smile to appear on our faces cannot be produced at will. These reactions can be activated by something within us or by a combination of internal and external causes and processes. For example, illness or injury can cause pain, and pain can activate anger, or fine food and wine can stimulate our physical sense of taste and in turn generate the emotion of happiness and well-being.

The online encyclopaedia, Wikipedia:

http://en.wikipedia.org/wiki/Emotions

has an exhaustive list of emotions. These include (in alphabetical order):

• Acceptance	• Amusement	• Anger	• Anticipation
• Calmness	• Comfort	• Confidence	• Cool
• Courage	• Depression	• Disgust	• Desire
• Envy	• Fear	• Friendship	• Grief
• Guilt	• Glee	• Gladness	• Hate
• Happiness	• Hope	• Joy	• Jealousy
• Kindness	• Love	• Pain	• Patience
• Phobia	• Rage	• Remorse	• Repentance
• Sadness	• Shame	• Sorrow	• Shock
• Suffering	• Surprise	• Terror	

Of course, some of these may well be different degrees of the same emotion – Gladness, Happiness and Joy are probably good examples of this. What is remarkable is that we can not only experience these different degrees of emotional reaction to events, but can recognise and calibrate the emotional reactions of others. We sense someone's happiness, can distinguish it from glee or joy, and can respond appropriately. In *'Emotions Revealed'*, the world renowned expert on body language, Paul Ekman, goes further in proposing that emotions actually determine the quality of our lives. He also suggests that while we don't always succeed, we organise our lives to maximise the experience of positive emotions and minimise the experience of negative emotions.

Modern neuroscience, with its increasing ability to see the brain at work as it processes information from our primary receptors (what we see with our eyes, touch with our bodies, hear with our ears, smell with our noses or taste with our mouths), indicates that we evaluate stimuli for their emotional significance as they travel along certain neural pathways to the limbic forebrain. What this means in practice is that we often react *emotionally* before we act *rationally* because it takes longer for us to process the information and reflect on it than it does for our emotional centres to respond. This is why emotional intelligence is so critical in decision-making. Our emotions will predispose us towards a particular event or set of behaviours by other people before our rational brain has fully evaluated the situation.

This was undoubtedly important when we were still living on the edge of survival in the early days of human development (hence the power of the 'fight or flight' reaction). Our bodies can help us to be prepared to react to save precious moments while we make sense of the threats or the dangers we face today. While the threats and the dangers are rarely of the same magnitude that our primitive forebears faced, the decisions we have to make are far more complex and can have significance far into the future. That's why it's so important to learn how to make sense of our own and others' emotional reactions as well apply rational logic to problems that we face.

Sensing others' emotions

So, emotions are part of our survival mechanism, as individuals and as a species, and they are accepted as vital because of that. Why then should we deny the effects of emotions in other settings? On a day-to-day basis, the organisational environment of leadership may not be as intense an emotional context as the life changing events of birth and death. However, a conscious and focused awareness of both our own and others' emotions plays a critical role in how we manage ourselves as well as how we communicate with others. Emotions shape our reactions to events and to people. What's more, we sense the emotions of others and these shape our own emotional reactions. If everyone about you is feeling despair, hostility, anger or fear, or exhilaration and happiness, then your own emotional reaction will be influenced without having to think about it. We instinctively sense the emotional environment and respond to it – this is what is meant by empathy.

Simon Baron-Cohen, a Cambridge Professor and co-director of the Autism Research Centre there, describes empathy in his book *The Essential Difference* (Allen Lane: 2003), as consisting of two components, one the cognitive, the other the affective. The cognitive component is the ability to understand other people's feelings and to take their perspective – to see and to feel things as they do. The affective component is the ability to respond with the appropriate emotion, like feeling sympathy for someone who has suffered bereavement.

The ability to empathise with others involves both components and it is a central argument of Baron-Cohen's book that women are, on balance, more empathetic than men, whereas men are more 'systemising' than women. *Systemising* means having a stronger drive to analyse, explore and construct a system. This is an issue we return to later in **MINDCHANGE**, but you can explore your empathising (and systemising) quotients by taking Baron-Cohen's questionnaire, included in his book and also available on-line at:

http://www.guardian.co.uk/life/flash/page/0,13249,937836,00.html

The tendency for men to score lower than women on empathising and higher on systemising is based on averages. The majority of people, of course, score near the mean and there are many men who score higher on empathising than the average woman, just as there are many women who score higher on systemising than the average man. However, it could be interpreted to suggest that men are more likely to be attracted by the systems aspect of management and women by the people aspect (this is grossly over-simplifying, of course). As we shall show, effective leaders are also effective managers, and vice versa, so the challenge to both men and women is to develop both aspects of their cognitive and affective intellectual processes.

Leaders who do not recognise their own emotional reactions are unlikely to recognise the emotional reactions of others. Emotional insensitivity is as much a weakness for a leader as an inability to count would be for a statistician – being aware of and alert to the power of emotions is vital to the leadership role, and one that any leader needs to both recognise and practice to be an effective leader. Just as those statisticians who are particularly adept at analysing and using numbers are recognised as having a superior conceptual ability, so those leaders who are more able to recognise and use their own and others' emotions to achieve objectives are more effective leaders.

The hip-hop approach ~ tapping into bling

'I am the hip-hop generation and I am going to have an impact.'
Russell Simmons

'My dream is to become the first black President of the United States.'
Serena Royal

The Syracuse Hip-Hop Summit reported on by Joanna Walters in The Times (on the 8th April 2004) may seem an unlikely example to include as an example of emotional intelligence. However, the approach of Richard Simmons, a 46-year-old music mogul provides a consummate example of EQ in practice. Tapping into young and poor people's perceived sense of powerlessness in influencing political decisions and aiming to influence them to take part by using their votes in the presidential election, was his prime purpose for organising a 3-hour event combining rap music and debate in Syracuse, upstate New York in early 2004.

The opposite of passion being described as indifference applies as much to politics as it does to personal relationships, and Simmons effectively tapped into young peoples' feelings during the Hip-Hop Summit with a blend of rap music and evangelical fervour to inspire them into using the power of their votes. By acknowledging the struggle that he had gone through to

---

motivate himself into, to do something better than 'just sitting around' and by speaking to them in their own language, he inspired not only those who felt previously disconnected from the process to go out and vote, but also the above quote from Serena Royal.

Recognising their perceived sense of hopelessness and wanting to persuade the next generation to use their vote when he had been too apathetic to use his, was a driving force behind his campaign. 'You can't get no bling-bling long-term unless you give something to the community', was part of his rallying cry to the massed audience of young people; an assertion that endorses not only political involvement but community spirit and a sense of responsibility that fits the emotional integrity element of EQ.

The EQ process of self-awareness, awareness of others, reflection and application (explained in more detail later in **MINDCHANGE**) are all in place in Simmons's self declared 'integrationist' approach. An endorsement of his ability to reach across divides between race, religion and political beliefs by Bakari Kitwana, author of *'The Crisis in African American Culture'* is testament to Simmons's effectiveness. A leadership example that no doubt, politicians of all nationalities and managers at all levels could learn EQ lessons from!

Intelligences explored

Conventionally, we think of intelligence as primarily comprising intellectual abilities such as analysing numerical data, using language to develop logical arguments, appreciating spatial relationships or applying reasoning to complex problems. In reality, there is far more to intelligence than these particular abilities. Harvard psychologist Howard Gardner has developed a theory of multiple intelligences that has become increasingly accepted as a more satisfactory explanation of intelligence than the more limited model that has dominated our understanding to date.

Gardner argues that there are at least seven possible intelligences (or perhaps dimensions of intelligence):

- visual/spatial
- musical
- verbal
- logical/mathematical
- interpersonal
- intrapersonal (e.g. insight, meta-cognition – the ability to 'think about thinking')
- bodily/kinaesthetic.

The traditional model of intelligence focuses on a limited number of these dimensions, especially the verbal and the logical/mathematical. But think of those people who have spectacular artistic abilities, or can learn and use other languages with ease, or craft objects of great beauty from coarse pieces of wood or metal. Why not recognise these abilities as a form of intelligence by acknowledging that those who exhibit insight into their own and others emotions, and who are able to employ that knowledge to shape their own and other's behaviour, also exhibit a specific intelligence – emotional intelligence?

There is then the problem of the assumption that intelligence is something we are born with and there is little that we can do to improve it. An alternative view is that a person's intelligence (however it is defined) is affected by a wide range of environmental and experiential factors, from education and nutrition through to the influence of relationships during formative years. It is probably more accurate to say that we have a potential which may or may not be fulfilled, and that whilst there may be an upper limit to this potential, most of us probably fail to reach that.

With regard to the development of emotional intelligence, a research report written by Mark Slaski of the University of Manchester Institute of Science and Technology (presented at the British Psychological Society's Occupational Psychology Conference in 2001) found evidence not only that people with high EQ are more likely to make good managers, but that managers can be taught to think and behave in a more emotionally intelligent way. While EQ as a specific component of training and development programmes is still in its infancy, our experience of working with clients on the development of EQ and how it relates to effective leadership and teamwork supports these findings, not only that EQ can be developed, but that its development can also make a real and positive difference. Furthermore, the emergence of emotional intelligence as a concept and the growing recognition of its value, has increasingly legitimised emotions as an important part of thinking and a fundamental part of the value system that guides us.

Twenty years ago Edward de Bono's best selling book *'Six Thinking Hats'* emphasised the importance of emotions and their effect on our decision making. He suggested that in a normal business discussion you are not supposed to allow your emotions to enter in, but goes on to argue that *'they enter in anyway – you merely disguise them as logic.'* De Bono used the idea of different coloured hats as a metaphor to encourage managers and leaders to recognise that there are different ways of thinking about problems. By employing different ways of thinking, we look at problems from a different perspective and generate different solutions as a result.

De Bono suggests that the *'red hat'* (which he calls the emotional 'thinking hat)', allows the thinker to legitimise emotions and feelings as an important part of thinking and to say openly, *'This is how I feel about the matter.'* He also proposes that one of the benefits of *'red hat'* thinking is that it makes feelings visible so that they become part of the thinking *'map'* and part of the value system that chooses a route on that map.

As passionate believers in the value of emotional intelligence and its application, let us present two of our favourite quotes from the book.

'In the end, all decisions are really 'red hat'. We lay out the factors but the final decision is emotional.'

'Any good decision must be emotional in the end ...when we have used thinking to make the map, our choice of route is determined by values and emotions.'

Body and mind

But emotions and emotional intelligence have a profound significance in areas other than management and leadership. Emotions don't just shape our ability to relate to other people and make management decisions, they also affect our health. On November 23rd 2003, John Elliot wrote a report in *The Times* about a two-day conference on the science of wellbeing hosted by the Royal Society (described as 'Britain's most august scientific body') that highlighted the change of thinking in the medical world about the importance of emotions.

Elliot quoted Dr Nick Baylis, a Cambridge University psychologist and one of the conference organisers, commenting that *'For the Royal Society to give us its countenance is vital, because that states that what we are doing deserves to be acknowledged and investigated by the best scientific minds'.* The focus of the conference was research findings about happiness and its significance in general wellbeing, emphasising the indisputable link between emotions and our physical state. A regular update can be found in his column in the *Saturday Times Magazine*, written under the heading *'Dr Feelgood – on the science of happiness.'*

The mind-body connection and its impact on our immune system as well as our energy levels can be profound. Research into the mind (psychology), the brain (neurology) and the body's natural defence system (immunology) is now a rapidly emerging field of study, referred to as psychoneuroimmunology (abbreviated to PNI). Research into wellbeing plus that concerning our neurological cognitive processes – how the brain actually works in other words – will undoubtedly make a significant contribution to our understanding of emotional intelligence and its importance in shaping our behaviour and relationships.

Personality, character and emotions

Clearly there are links between personality, emotions and emotional intelligence, but to understand those links, we need to understand what we mean by 'personality'. For years, personality has largely been defined by reference to four factors; for example, the Myers-Briggs personality typology measures people as being either extrovert or introvert, sensing or intuitive, thinking or feeling, and using judgement or perception. This approach recognises that each pair comprises two ends of a continuum but assumes that people lie at one end or another and so can fall into one or other category (i.e. either introvert or extrovert).

However, recent developments in our understanding of the psychology of personality have moved away from this model to a five-factor model (outlined below), each factor of which can then be broken down into smaller dimensions (although there isn't always agreement about what they are!). The emerging new approach to personality is not a radical departure but more of an evolution. Instead of four there are now believed to be five dimensions of personality, and measures of people's personality along each dimension are likely to be spread in a normal distribution rather than lying to one end or the other (what's called a 'bimodal distribution'). This means the majority will be grouped closely together in the centre, exhibiting no strong preference for one or other extreme.

Therefore, instead of personality types linking extremes of personality on each dimension in different combinations, the emphasis is on individual personality traits, indicated by the strength of someone's score on each dimension.

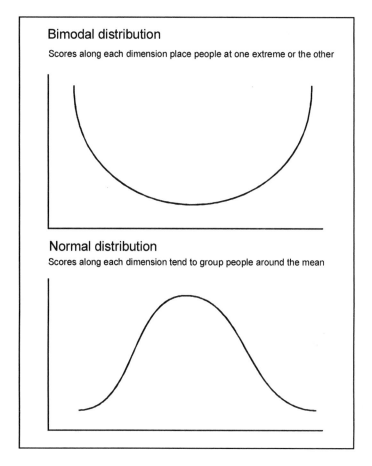

*The change in emphasis in how personality is measured
along each dimension*

Perhaps, most significantly, the five-factor approach is based on experience, not theory. That is, it derives from observation and experimentation, rather than a set of theoretical assumptions about how personality is determined.

Of course, just to make life difficult for those trying to understand the significance of emotions in our lives, psychologists are not agreed on the exact nature of the big five (for example, Costa and McCrae's

'OCEAN model' of personality consists of Openness, Conscientiousness, Extraversion, Agreeableness and Neuroticism, which are similar to but use different labels for, the five dimensions below). So, these five following dimensions describe a widely but not universally accepted version of the big five.

1. Negative Emotionality (or Neuroticism)

Negative Emotionality – or the 'N' Factor – assesses how easily we respond to environmental stimuli. Some people get upset or angry very easily, reflecting a high 'N' factor. This is clearly closely related to people's emotional intelligence, especially their ability to manage their emotions.

2. Extraversion

How extrovert or introvert people are – the 'E' Factor. This assesses how much people enjoy being with other people and being actively engaged with them. There is no obvious causal link with emotional intelligence – introverts and extroverts may equally be very emotionally aware or lack the social skills to recognise emotions in others.

3. Originality (or Openness to different interests)

This is the 'O' Factor – how open we are to different interests. People with a high 'O' Factor will do lots of things, but not in as much depth as people with a low 'O' factor who will be highly involved with few interests.

4. Accommodation (or Agreeableness)

This is the 'A' Factor – how accommodating we are to alternative attitudes, values and points of view. People with a high 'A' Factor will accept a wide range, whereas those with a low 'A' factor will tend to have strong opinions and not listen to others. It is probable that a high 'A' Factor will encourage greater emotional intelligence, as people have to be more alert to others' emotions in relating to them.

5. Consolidation (or Conscientiousness)

The 'C' Factor – how conscientious we are, committed and organised to do something. People with high 'C' Factor will get on and do what they say they are going to do, whereas people with a low 'C' Factor can be unreliable.

Most of us tend towards the middle of this range, and are able to be more organised, get things done and meet our commitments when we feel motivated to do so. We can be highly organised for short periods and occasionally just let things slide when we lack any strong engagement with the task. As a manager and leader, you will find high 'C' Factor people easier to manage but sometimes inflexible, whereas low 'C' Factor people drive you mad until you need something done urgently, when they will drop everything and get stuck in when a short burst of activity is needed.

The central majority

Although it is assumed that personality is hard-wired – that it is a fixed feature of us as individuals – there is evidence that from adolescence to early adult life our personality does change. Primarily N (Negative Emotionality), E (how extrovert we are), and O (how open we are to different interests) tend to decrease, and A (how accommodating we are to alternative attitudes, values and points of view) and C (how conscientious we are, committed and organised we are) tend to increase.

In other words, we become less driven by our emotional reactions and more detached, more introspective, less open to different interests and more focused, and also more accommodating and conscientious. Perhaps most importantly, this tendency is greater amongst those in full time work (rather than in full time education, for example). This is important, not least because it tells us that personality is at least partly determined by our social environment, and also because it identifies some important differences between different age groups in the way they are likely to respond to their environment.

Furthermore, although personality is about a set of largely stable traits, as well as there being some change during early adulthood, most of us are able to act in ways that run contrary to our personalities if we concentrate and have a good reason for doing so, at least for short periods or in limited contexts. Personality is therefore about tendencies, not railway tracks that we are programmed to follow.

Do you recognise yourself or any of your work colleagues in any of these descriptions of personality traits? The one important thing to remember is that these are all about dimensions where it is easiest to describe the few at either end of the spectrum and not the many who cluster around the centre. It's also important to remember that it is a very small minority who lie at all the extremes and have the kind of personalities that are very hard to cope with, whichever extreme it is.

As a rule, people in leadership and management roles are likely to be in the position of supervising people younger than themselves, including some who are recent entrants to the workforce. If you are in this position, it's helpful to consciously recognise that the way younger people react to events may well differ from your reactions due to this maturation effect. They may seem more emotional about events and express their emotions more because of their greater extroversion. They may seem to be more divergent (less consistent) in their interests. They may also be more dogmatic in their tendency to see only 'one right way' and be less committed to their work or the organisation.

One aspect of emotional intelligence is to recognise that other people's behaviour is driven by other concerns than your own, and that what seems right and appropriate to you may not seem right and appropriate to them. Recognising that this is a feature of everybody's individuality (rather than a deliberate attempt to be awkward!) is an important step in developing your emotional intelligence. Personality is a key dimension of individuality – it is central to making someone the person he or she is – and being alert to different personality traits and the behaviour that may arise as a result is part of being more emotionally intelligent.

Although personality may predispose us to behave in certain ways, it doesn't drive us to do so (other than in a small minority of extreme personality types). Most of us are capable of developing behaviours which may not come to us naturally but which will produce more positive results for us and for others. Using and developing our emotional intelligence is one really effective way of doing this, because emotional intelligence emphasises awareness of our own feelings and the feelings that others have. The more adept we get at recognising these, the better we will be able to relate to others and to make an impact.

People who are introverted will probably lack confidence in their ability to lead others, whereas extroverts may over estimate their ability. Emotional intelligence encourages us to recognise what we are capable of and what is holding us back, and helps us to fulfil our potential. Equally it makes us alert to others and helps to stop us over-estimating our ability to lead others towards our goals.

Origins of the EQ concept

'We should take care not to make intellect our god. It has of course powerful muscles, but no personality.'
Einstein

So far we've talked about emotions and their importance in our social interactions. We've also looked at how personality and our ability to empathise shapes our relationships with others and at the various traits that define our individual personalities. Throughout all this we have alluded to 'emotional intelligence' without being explicit as to what it is. We will rectify that now, before moving on to consider how our ability to lead and manage others is defined, at least in part, by our emotional intelligence. We will then look at what we can do to develop and improve this elusive quality.

But we will start with a brief overview to show how emotional intelligence as a concept has developed and used to help make sense of the complexity of human interaction.

Mayer and Salovey

John D. Mayer of the University of New Hampshire is credited, along with Peter Salovey of Yale University, with having come up with the emotional intelligence theory in the 1980s in their studies of the interaction between emotion and cognition. They first published articles describing the concept in 1990, and it was one of these ('Emotional intelligence' in *Imagination, Cognition and Personality* volume 9) that first, in John Mayer's own words:

'attracted the most attention by far. This article presents our first model of emotional intelligence. It is also the article most heavily relied upon by Goleman in his first book. The article provided an

overview of research in a number of (then) apparently unrelated areas and suggested that findings from those different areas indicated the presence of a coherent ability: emotional intelligence.'

As they refined their model, so others developed similar (or competing) versions, like Daniel Goleman, who Mayer refers to above. The Mayer and Salovey Four Branch Model of Emotional Intelligence is explained in detail in their various books, and (as its name suggests) comprises four main categories (or branches) which are then sub-divided into specific dimensions:

The Mayer and Salovey Four Branch Model of Emotional Intelligence

I - Emotional Perception and Expression	II - Emotional Facilitation of Thought
• Ability to identify emotion in one's physical and psychological states. • Ability to identify emotion in other people. • Ability to express emotions accurately and to express needs related to them. • Ability to discriminate between accurate/honest and inaccurate/dishonest feelings.	• Ability to redirect and prioritise thinking on the basis of associated feelings. • Ability to generate emotions to facilitate judgment and memory. • Ability to capitalise on mood changes to appreciate multiple points of view. • Ability to use emotional states to facilitate problem-solving and creativity.

III. Emotional Understanding	IV. Emotional Management
• Ability to understand relationships among various emotions. • Ability to perceive the causes and consequences of emotions. • Ability to understand complex feelings, emotional blends, and contradictory states. • Ability to understand transitions among emotions.	• Ability to be open to feelings, both pleasant and unpleasant. • Ability to monitor and reflect on emotions. • Ability to engage, prolong, or detach from an emotional state. • Ability to manage emotions in oneself. • Ability to manage emotions in others.

The first of these branches, Emotional Perception and Expression, is essentially a form of emotional literacy and begs the questions *'Can you recognise your own and other's emotional states?'* and *'Can you describe your own emotions and can you discriminate between true and false emotions?'* Without this basic emotional literacy, we'd be lost in a world where emotions shape so much of our daily lives, including our working lives.

The second of these branches of emotional intelligence, in Mayer and Salovey's Four Branch Model, is the ability to use emotional intelligence, to turn the tables on traditional emotional control mechanisms. Whereas emotions can over-ride rational analysis, emotionally intelligent people can employ their understanding of their emotions to make more informed decisions and behave more effectively. There is plenty of evidence that the best decision-making in the workplace is informed by emotional sensitivity, since understanding how people will respond to a decision is an essential element of the decision-making process.

Emotionally intelligent people will allow their emotions to influence their decision-making in a balanced way, drawing on their emotions to make sense of their own thinking and to shape their approaches to problem solving and decision-making.

The third branch of the Mayer and Salovey model is our ability to understand how our emotions relate to and interact with each other, and the complex reactions we may experience which arise from these interactions. Think of the reaction that people have when they hear that someone they dislike (an emotion) suffers a personal mishap and is clearly very unhappy (an emotion). The response may well mix up a sense of (perhaps slight!) pleasure (an emotion) at their suffering, tinged with sympathy (an emotion) coloured by guilt (an emotion) about the pleasure, leading to resentment (an emotion) at being made to feel guilty! (The Germans have a word for extremes of this – *schadenfreude*)

Emotionally intelligent people recognise these emotions and that they are interacting, and the way in which they lead on to other emotions, because, of course, the resentment can further reinforce the dislike that triggered the complex emotions in the first place!

The final branch, the fourth, is the ability to manage these emotional reactions. This means accepting that they have the effect they do, recognising when emotions occur and taking charge rather than allowing them to take over.

It's clear that Mayer and Salovey's model represents a hierarchy, moving from emotional literacy (recognition) through the use of emotions, to an understanding leading on to management. Without the first element there would be no application. Without application, we can't develop an understanding, and without that understanding we can't manage our own and others' emotions.

But once Mayer and Salovey first unveiled their ideas, the floodgates seemed to open. In particular, there was a lot of emphasis on the role of emotional intelligence at work. Although the four elements in Mayer and Salovey's model are applicable to the workplace, they were concerned with emotional intelligence in its widest settings.

35

Cooper and Sawaf

Amongst those who concentrated on the workplace, Robert Cooper and Ayman Sawaf have been particularly influential. They carried out research in the USA on emotions at work and developed what they call 'the 4 cornerstones' of emotional intelligence. They describe these as:

- **Emotional Literacy:** Being true and real to yourself, building personal power through self-awareness, inner guidance, respect, responsibility and connection. This is the ability to recognise and understand one's own emotions, and is similar to Mayer and Salovey's *Emotional Perception and Expression.*

- **Emotional Fitness:** Being clear and getting along with others, to inspire oneself and others through authenticity, resilience and trusting relationships. This is the ability to relate to others and understand their emotions, and is not dissimilar to *Emotional Understanding.*

- **Emotional Depth:** Reaching down into one's inner self to build one's core character and show integrity and purpose. This is the ability to develop and build one's own strength of character to become more effective in relationships with others. This has similarities to *Emotional Facilitation of Thought.*

- **Emotional Alchemy:** Sensing opportunities and creating the future rather than letting it happen, being intuitive and innovative, integrating ideas to make sense of situations and resolve problems. This is about using the knowledge of oneself and others, through one's own personal strength, to shape the world we inhabit rather than allowing it to shape you, like Mayer and Salovey's *Emotional Management.*

Cooper and Sawaf's published their findings under the title *'Executive EQ – emotional intelligence in business'*, in 1997. But they are not alone. Other leading researchers and writers on the subject include Anabel Jensen (the author of four books on teaching and learning EQ), Esther Orioli (author of the *'EQ Map'*), Geetu Bharwaney (author of *'Emotionally Intelligent Living'*) and David Caruso.

Higgs and Dulewicz

Although most of the research has been carried out in the USA, Malcolm Higgs and Vic Dulewicz at Henley Management College also examined the phenomenon here in the UK during the 1990s. Findings from their research about leadership competence and success supported previous USA research.

> What makes their conclusions particularly useful is that they propose that emotional competence, (i.e. a high level EQ, suggesting that people have well developed emotional intelligence) is a more important factor in successful leadership than traditional success measures. In particular, they identified three key components of emotional intelligence producing this superior performance:
>
> - **Drivers** - the motivation and decisiveness that energise goal achievement
> - **Constrainers** - the conscientiousness and integrity that facilitates the fit between principles, values and behaviour; and
> - **Enablers** - the performance traits which contribute to success, such as sensitivity, influence and self-awareness.

Malcolm Higgs emphasises how important it is for leaders to manage their own emotions and to be aware of others' emotions as well. Emotionally intelligent leadership is, he argues, about *'achieving one's goals through the ability to manage one's own feelings and emotions, being sensitive to and influencing other key people, and balancing one's own motives and drives with conscientious and ethical behaviour'*.

Goleman

However, it is Daniel Goleman who is usually credited with popularising the term 'Emotional Intelligence', following the publication of his book of the same name, in 1995. Goleman has described emotionally adept people as those who *'know and manage their own feelings well, and who deal effectively with other people's feelings'*. For him, the main components of this emotional intelligence are:

- self-awareness
- 'emotional management'
- self-motivation
- empathy
- managing relationships
- communication skills
- personal style.

Goleman has argued that emotional intelligence is probably one of, if not the, most important factor in determining success at work, particularly for what he calls 'star performers', those who rise to the top and stand out amongst their peers. Why? Because it is emotional intelligence that enables people to convert what they and others know into action, through their ability to build relationships and influence others, based on their own self-knowledge.

What you will notice in looking at Goleman's model is that it is not really confined to the emotional spectrum – concepts like self-motivation and communication skills extend into the cognitive domain and into personality characteristics. These are obviously related to emotions, in that they predispose us to react emotionally to a greater or lesser extent, but it does confuse the issue a little – are we talking about people's ability to recognise, use, understand and manage their emotions, as Mayer and Salovey first introduced the concept or are we including character traits that Mayer and Salovey insist should be distinguished from its definition?

(For further reading on the conceptualisation and development of emotional intelligence theory and its measurement and application, *'Key Readings on the Mayer and Salovey Model'*, edited by Salovey, Brackett and Mayer, published in the USA by Dude Publishing, provides an authoritative and in-depth guide.)

What does it all mean?

The practice of being emotionally intelligent (or not!) has existed since people first interacted with each other. It's the recognition of emotional intelligence and the use of the specific term that has only been in place since the 1980s. To confuse matters slightly, 'emotional intelligence' is also referred to as *'Emotional quotient'* (EQ), and both terms tend to be used interchangeably.

An example of this inter-changeability of the term is 'Nexus EQ' (based in the USA), an organisation created in 2000 by a team of emotional intelligence experts and leaders working in collaboration. Nexus EQ:

http://www.nexuseq.com/

was set up specifically to improve performance, enhance leadership and increase learning by sharing ideas and best practice in emotional intelligence.

Strictly defined however, 'EQ' is a *measure* or *quotient* of emotional intelligence, in the same way that IQ is a measure of general intelligence. Despite this, from a theoretical standpoint, it seems logical to make the link between emotional intelligence and the competencies that demonstrate its application. Emphasising the distinction between emotional intelligence ('EI') and EQ is important nevertheless, in reflecting on the two factors involved in measuring someone's EQ, i.e.:

1. what you are measuring
2. how you measure it.

In order to have any real confidence in the measurement of EQ we have to have some agreement about the emotional intelligence that is being measured, and then develop instruments that are sensitive enough to measure it. At the moment, the agreement on the meaning of emotional intelligence is still far off, with so many different perspectives and models around that it makes it difficult to make sense of them all, let alone have confidence in the EQ measures being used. In practice, many of the different models have a strong similarity, offering slight variants on the same basic themes. Before we look at how to measure EQ, we are going to look first at some of the more significant ideas in order to make some sense of the basic concept. This will help us to identify the core themes that can help anyone to improve their leadership abilities by using and developing their emotional intelligence.

What do we mean by leadership abilities?

The plethora of writers on the subject of leadership includes: Warren Bennis, Burt Nanus, James Champy, Howard Gardner and Peter Drucker. Warren Bennis referred to six 'basic ingredients' of leadership, which he listed as: guiding vision, passion, integrity, trust, curiosity and seven 'Megaskills' of leadership: farsightedness, mastery of change, organisation design, anticipatory learning, initiative, mastery of interdependence and high standards of integrity. James Champy emphasises cultural conditions of relentless pursuit, creative thinking and teamwork, while Peter Drucker asserts that the attributes demonstrated by different leaders are so many and varied, that he refutes the idea of fundamental leadership characteristics and traits.

According to Joseph Boyett and Jimmie Boyett's *'The Guru Guide - the best ideas of the top management thinkers'*, what is generally agreed is that the one characteristic that separates leaders from non-leaders is that they have 'willing followers'. Leadership abilities can therefore be defined as those that enable people to create 'followership' - that is, leaders inspire others to want to follow the route they have carved out. The key phrase here is 'want to'.

Forcing people down a particular road is not leadership, but creating a real desire to follow that route is.

Given this, we believe that leadership involves the ability to:·

- conceive a vision for where you want to be, based on your core values and beliefs, and communicate that vision to people in a way that convinces them to buy into this
- see the abilities in people that they may not themselves recognise and allow them the opportunity to grow and develop these
- be aware of your own strengths and weaknesses, and welcome the contribution of others to compensate for your limitations
- demonstrate honesty and integrity in words and deeds
- agree goals with people that are achievable yet stretch them to fulfil their potential, commit yourself to similar goals and work to fulfil your commitments
- instil a sense of shared commitment with others towards the achievement of goals
- recognise the barriers that prevent people from achieving their goals and help them to overcome these
- be honest about your own achievements and welcome feedback from others so that you learn
- be prepared to adapt to changing circumstances
- win with magnanimity, lose with good grace.

The power of intuition

One significant characteristic of people with a high EQ is their level of intuition, which can play a key role in how effectively they manage both their business and personal relationships. In *'Executive EQ'*, Cooper and Sawaf (1997) define intuition as *'direct knowing without the conscious use of reasoning'* and suggest that we do not become whole and successful until our intuition is playing an integral role in guiding our decisions. In other words, it is acknowledging that the initial emotional reaction to any stimulus can be as important in shaping our behaviour as the rational analysis that follows. (Neuroscientists suggest that intuition can be thought of as unmediated emotional response which has as much legitimacy as a more rational, analytical response for those who are emotionally aware.)

Robert Cooper and Ayman Sawaf, who identified the four cornerstones, define emotional intelligence as:

'The ability to sense, understand and effectively apply the power and acumen of emotions as a source of human energy, information, connection and influence.'

The founding fathers of emotional literacy, John Mayer and Peter Salovey, first described it as:

'The ability to perceive, to integrate, to understand and reflectively manage one's own and other people's feelings.'

Their revised definition (included in *'Key Readings on the Mayer and Salovey Model'* 2004) provides a more comprehensive explanation:

'Emotional intelligence involves the ability to perceive accurately, appraise and express emotion; the ability to access and/or generate feelings when they facilitate thought; the ability to understand emotion and emotional knowledge; and the ability to regulate emotions to promote educational and intellectual growth.'

While definitions may vary in emphasis and expression, the core elements of emotional intelligence come through quite clearly, especially as the concept applies to the work environment, as:

- acknowledging and understanding one's own emotions and the way that these are expressed to others, both verbally and non-verbally

- listening to and reflecting on one's intuitive feelings *(gut reactions)*

- being aware of others' body language and behaviours, interpreting and anticipating their emotions

- responding with appropriate behaviour to own and others' emotions within an ethical framework of principles and values.

The definition of emotional intelligence that underpins **MINDCHANGE**, as originally outlined by Jan Childs in 1998, and which makes central the role of emotional intelligence in shaping leadership behaviour, summarises these elements. Emotional intelligence is:

'Acknowledging and understanding the influence of emotions on ourselves and others, and responding using integrity and intuition to guide behaviour.'

EQ4U – Developing Emotional Competence

*'Emotional intelligence is a short cut to achievement, but
there's no short cut to achieving it.'*
Dr. Malaa Kapadia
Indian professor, former journalist and HR practitioner –
responsible for pioneering research on emotional intelligence
in the Indian context

Looking at these different approaches to leadership and the abilities
involved, they all have some common themes and underpinning
concepts. The difficulty is to translate them into a model for
operational leadership – for actually doing something practical with
the idea of Emotional Intelligence. For that reason, **MINDCHANGE**
offers you a process for developing your EQ, and not simply a
description of what emotional intelligence is. This is what we call
EQ4U. It's a four-stage process, starting with you and finishing with
action by you.

Given that there are already so many different models about, why
develop another one? For a start, a number of the models attempt to
describe a range of abilities or dimensions of emotional intelligence,
not a process for applying it. Secondly, the implications of some of
these are that emotional intelligence represents some kind of static
phenomenon – that emotional intelligence is like conventional
intelligence, a quality that you are born with and that you either
cannot change or have limited ability to do so.

The purpose of **EQ4U** is not to describe emotional intelligence but
to help you apply your EQ and, through application, develop it. There
is evidence that conventional intelligence is not a fixed quantum that
people are born with, but something that can be developed or

hindered in its development by a wide range of environmental conditions. For example, Dr Dennis Garlick of Sydney University, writing in the American Psychological Association's *Psychological Review* in 2002, analysed some 124 reports of research and concluded that a variety of environmental factors determined how far people were able to develop their intellectual abilities to their full potential. We believe that EQ can be developed or hindered as well. That's not the same as saying that everyone is capable of achieving the same level of emotional intelligence, rather that emotional intelligence is an ability that degrades if not exercised and is enhanced by practice, whatever base you start from. **EQ4U** is designed as a simple but effective set of stages that you can work through when addressing any issue involving yourself and/or others that harness your emotional intelligence to best effect.

There are four steps to **EQ4U** starting with your own self-awareness and understanding, moving on to consider your awareness and understanding of others, then to reflection and finally to application through action. It is not about abstractions but about the employment of skills and practices that can enhance your ability to work with others, to manage them and to lead them. Part Four - 'Developing EQ Leadership' explains in more detail how you can develop your emotional competence. The following outline will help you to understand what **EQ4U** is about. The rest of **MINDCHANGE** shows you how it can be used to understand how people and organisations behave.

Step 1: Self-awareness and understanding

Step one is about being prepared to listen to and reflect on your intuitive feelings (your gut reactions). What do you really feel about the issue you are facing or the problem you are dealing with? This doesn't mean ignoring objective facts or collecting information to help you make better decisions, it just means not ignoring the feelings that you have as well.

You also need to be aware of your inner body language 'signals' and associated emotions, and acknowledge that these may well tell you something about your own feelings that you are trying to suppress. Awareness of the signals you are giving to others by more visible body language is also important in self-awareness; perhaps your body language means they may well be deciding more accurately than you are, what you are thinking and feeling without being aware of it yourself? Improving your self-awareness is the first step to raising your EQ. If you don't know yourself then you will never fully know others and what they may be thinking and feeling.

Step 2: Awareness and understanding of others

Being interested in other people, what they are thinking and feeling, and aware of their body language and behaviours is Step 2. How do people react to you? Do they look you in the eye, do they seem pleased if you take an interest in what they are doing, do they relax when you are present? Or do they avoid direct eye contact, do they look worried when you appear and tense up, suddenly trying to look busy so you'll pass them by?

To be emotionally intelligent, you need to be able to interpret and anticipate other peoples' emotions, taking account of the particular situation you are in. Interpreting means looking at what people do and how they do it. Think of some of the emotions we listed earlier, such as Amusement or Anger, Confidence or Depression, Fear or Friendship. Just imagine the range of physical expressions that people make of those different emotions and the contrast between the pairs. Recognising these emotions, understanding what is generating them and anticipating how and when they may occur is a key element of the EQ process. Leadership means being able to interpret them, recognise and understand them, and to anticipate when they are likely to occur so that you can prepare for them or take steps to avert them, if appropriate.

We call these first two **EQ4U** stages the 'red light phase', because of the importance of stopping and focusing on your own and others' emotional reactions. Any sensible driver stops at a red light, just as sensible, emotionally intelligent managers and leaders stop to check how they are feeling and observe the signs from others to identify their feelings as well.

Step 3: Reflection

This third stage of **EQ4U** we refer to as the 'amber phase' - still maintaining caution but getting ready to act. Leadership means taking people forward, even when there are no rules or procedures to guide you. All that you have are the principles and values that you manage your own life by. Understanding the ethical framework of principles and values that shape your judgements and decisions is fundamental to emotional intelligence. Reflection starts with looking in at yourself and asking searching questions about why you do things the way you do and what values and principles really guide your life.

As well as looking in on yourself (emotionally intelligent leadership can be described as an 'inside out' approach), it's also about reflecting on the overall situation, including your own and others' circumstances. What has caused this situation to arise, why has it happened here, now? Reflection involves looking beyond the immediate situation to consider the past and its effect on the present.

From that you can then reflect on your own emotions and what you anticipate others' emotions are likely to be. Our emotions are a product of more than the moment; they are the result of a complex series of interacting experiences that have conditioned us to react in a particular way. Two people who were once friends but have had a falling out will react very differently to an experience. When they were friends it might have been laughed at, now it may well cause anger and resentment. Understanding what shapes their emotional reaction – and yours – is fundamental to the EQ process.

Emotionally competent leaders reflect on how they communicate with others, to think before they speak. They choose words that show that they recognise and understand the context, so that they are clear in what they say and that their words are perceived as being appropriate to the situation. They always strive to be genuine, open and honest. That's only possible if they reflect carefully about what they really think and believe and if it fits with their value and belief system.

Finally, they ensure that their communication demonstrates an appropriate degree of warmth. What are they trying to communicate through their words? It's not just what they say but how they say it that counts. They reflect on the tone of their voice, their posture, their proximity to the people they are speaking to and their other body language, to make sure that they are being authentic and communicating the same message as their words.

These three steps – Self-awareness and understanding, Awareness and understanding of others, and Reflection – provide the precondition for step 4, Application, i.e. demonstrating emotional competence. This means responding to others with behaviour that reflects your own emotions and their emotional state, and matches the ethical principles and values that you regard as important. It also means communicating genuinely, openly and honestly. Developing your EQ is not quick, but that doesn't mean it's difficult, just demanding. Demanding because you have to be able to be brutally honest with yourself if you want to be honest to others, and because when you look deeply into yourself, your feelings and your values, you may not always like what you see.

The more open you are to yourself about how you feel, the easier it is to be open to others. Revealing your doubts and uncertainties is not a sign of weakness, although far too many people think it is. It becomes a weakness if it holds you back from acting. Making decisions on partial or conflicting information often means that you will have doubts about the validity of the decisions, and you should reveal those doubts. However, having revealed, them you should then make your decision and be prepared to carry it through. The critical thing is to distinguish between the uncertainties that lie behind the decisions and the conviction with which you carry out the course of action you have determined.

Step 4: Application

The final phase of the **EQ4U** process is move – now you have the 'green light' to act. Being aware of and reflecting on the meaning of your own and others' emotional states must lead to action if you want to be more emotionally competent. This is action that is informed by these insights into your own and others' emotions and feelings, attitudes and values. It is also action informed by analysis of the situation and by consideration of the options. **EQ4U** is not only about reacting with emotional awareness; it is about matching rational analysis with emotional analysis, so that you are more fully aware.

Whatever the problem, whatever the situation, whoever you are dealing with, always remembers to:

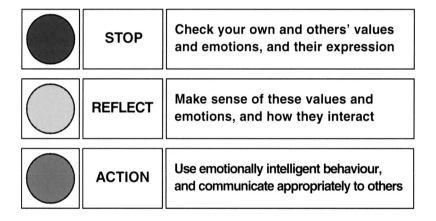

	STOP	Check your own and others' values and emotions, and their expression
	REFLECT	Make sense of these values and emotions, and how they interact
	ACTION	Use emotionally intelligent behaviour, and communicate appropriately to others

There are more details about each stage and the behaviours involved in developing emotionally intelligent leadership in Part 4 of **MINDCHANGE**.

Reflections Explored
Part 2:
The Leadership Dimension

Why EQ Matters to Organisations

*'Leadership is a potent combination of strategy and character.
But if you must be without one, be without the strategy.'*
General H Norman Schwarzkopf
(US leader of coalition forces in the first Gulf War)

For years writers and researchers looking at organisational performance and the role of managers and leaders have supported the value of applied emotional intelligence. For example, findings presented at a British Psychological Society conference in January 2001 and reported on by Elizabeth Judge in *The Times*, found a direct correlation with level of emotional intelligence and ratings of best management performance.

Many leading commentators on organisational leadership have expressed the same idea. The late Mark McCormack, when interviewed on the David Frost programme in 2000, said that *'Understanding human dynamics is still the most important thing in business'*. This emphasis on the importance of effective people relationships reflects what he wrote in 1994 in *'What They Don't Teach You at Harvard Business School'*, by challenging the rational, analytical view of management and leadership that is central to Harvard's (and many other universities') MBA programmes.

James Champy, one of the two leaders (with Mike Hammer) of the business process re-engineering revolution in the early nineties, goes further in emphasising the fundamental management changes he believes are essential:

'Everyone must change. The change will go deeper than technique. It touches not merely what managers do but who they are. Not just their sense of the task but their sense of themselves. Not just what they know but what they think. Not just their way of seeing the world but their way of living in the world.'

'You don't know what you've got till it's gone...'

The best place to see the value of emotional intelligence is when it's missing! Gerald Ratner joined his family's business in 1966 and was made chief executive in 1984. In less than 10 years, he transformed it from a business with 130 stores and turnover of £13m to a plc with 2,500 stores, 25,000 employees and profits of £121m. But a disastrous few seconds during the course of a 30 minute speech to 6,000 directors at the Royal Albert Hall, when he described a sherry decanter as 'total crap', cost him his personal fortune, his job, wiped an estimated £500m off the company's value and turned the profits into a £122m loss.

This is a classic example of how a lack of emotional intelligence had a significant negative impact on both business image and performance. While Gerald Ratner's comment may have been tongue in cheek and not intended to cause offence, he showed a complete insensitivity to the feelings of his customers and to the staff and investors who relied on his business. People who could not afford to buy high quality goods could at least feel that they were fulfilling their lifestyle ambitions by buying Ratner's low cost decanters. Whatever one may feel about their taste or ambitions, these were important personal statements for them. In despising the products, he effectively indicated that he despised the people who bought them and, implicitly, those who sold the goods and the investors who enabled the company to operate.

Undoubtedly there are countless unrecorded examples of poor emotional competence by leaders at a number of levels. Many of these will have had some sort of negative impact on the culture and the productivity of organisations large and small. (Remember our reference to Surcon International research findings in 'Opening Reflections'?). Conversely, emotionally intelligent leadership can have a positive effect on both people and productivity. Examples of leadership and emotional competence, are included in Part 3 – Exploring Leadership Practice.

In **MINDCHANGE,** our emphasis is on awareness of how your own behaviour and words can have an impact on other people, and by reflective practice, how you can develop yourself so that your emotional impact brings about the positive outcomes you are trying to achieve. But it's not just at the top of organisations that emotional intelligence is critical. Organisations are all about people – without people they are useless buildings and equipment, producing nothing.

The organisation charts that are used to illustrate how the organisation is structured say nothing about the complex relationships between individuals that determine what is produced and how well it is done. These relationships are all shaped by the interplay of emotion between leaders and managers at all levels, and by the people they lead and manage. It's too easy to assume that effective organisational performance is the result of simply employing people with the right skill set and then telling them to get on with the job.

As the education level of the population rises and as people's expectations rise, they are becoming more demanding of their employers. They want to be recognised for the contribution they make and for their ideas to be listened to. Emotional intelligence is about understanding how people react to changes in their workplace and the effect of externalities on their lives. **MINDCHANGE** is all about how managers and leaders at all levels need to recognise, understand and respond positively to the emotions of the people they work with and create an organisation that is, in effect, emotionally intelligent as well.

It is through applied emotional intelligence that organisations can engender the trust that they depend on to build their customer base, to secure investment and to attract the employees they need to survive. As well as trust, organisations also need to be able to unleash the creativity and innovative potential of their people, which in turn requires that they can harness their emotional as well as their intellectual abilities.

Organisational ethics, trust and EQ

One way in which organisations can encourage their employees' (and their customers' and other stakeholders') emotional engagement is through their ethical or values-based relationship with society, as well as their economic or transactional relationship. The transactional relationship is based on an exchange of goods and services based on satisfying mutual needs. These will be monetary exchanges to enable organisations to make a profit (or if they are in the public sector, to maximise service outcomes or take-up). The ethical or values-based relationship is about the organisation demonstrating a wider social responsibility, recognising obligations beyond the purely transactional ones.

Anita Roddick, founder of Body Shop, describes corporate social responsibility (CSR) as 'being better by being values-led' rather than by getting bigger and bigger. In her view, corporate social responsibility cannot be a 'mild form of the status quo', which she sees as focusing on making money. Though not in itself anti-capitalist, she envisages corporate social responsibility as demanding wider priorities. Those organisations that take a narrower view of corporate social responsibility still see their obligations as stretching beyond their purely economic objectives, as reflecting a need to be corporate citizens with social as well as an economic role in society.

Of course, corporate social responsibility isn't new. Victorian Quaker entrepreneurs like Fry, Rowntree and Cadbury practised CSR principles and the Co-operative Movement was founded on them. Body Shop has for years been an international leader in responsible sourcing of materials, both in terms of their environmental sustainability and the social and economic welfare of the communities providing them.

According to Diana Thomas, writing in the Institute of Leadership and Management magazine *Edge* in 2000, *'what has brought CSR to prominence now is a combination of several factors. First is a major shift of emphasis in the role of government. Successive UK governments have had a deliberate policy of 'exiting' from large areas of social responsibility. This role has been taken by business, and they are expected to operate with something approaching the same principles as the public sector organisations they have replaced.'*

Alongside this shift of responsibility has gone a shift in power. As Diana Thomas continues, *'On a global scale it is now the big corporations not national governments, which are most able to determine the economic success or failure of whole countries.'* But with that power has to come some responsibility for the actions that companies take, because their actions affect thousands, if not millions of people. Barclays Bank in apartheid South Africa, Shell in the Ogoniland area of Nigeria, Union Carbide in Bhopal, are all large companies that have seen their prestige and their image in the market damaged by their corporate activities. Their decisions have affected large numbers of people who were unable to have a voice in the decision-making process that caused those companies to take the actions they did.

What is all too often apparent is that the leadership of many organisations lacks the emotional competence to recognise how their actions will affect others. Perhaps the most significant areas of current concern are the resistance to GM crops that has led companies like Monsanto to be vilified for their involvement and commitment to their development, and fears about climate change and the apparent reluctance of oil giant Exxon to acknowledge the potential effect. From the outside, these large corporations appear monolithic and impersonal, driven by people who don't seem to share the concerns of many looking in from the outside. What is sought so often is an acknowledgement that those concerns are legitimate and that people have a right to have them examined and responded to.

Some companies have responded to these concerns by setting up corporate social responsibility units, developing policies on the environment, on ethics, on the use of child labour, etc. But this is often viewed cynically by observers as the result of external pressure and a fig leaf to hide their true agenda. To a large extent, this reflects an increasing lack of trust, in business, in government and the various institutions that have for so long been given wide responsibility for areas like the law, medicine and education.

Integrity matters

Trust implies a degree of certainty about a person or an organisation's future behaviour. It combines elements of objective analysis of past and current performance, particularly seeking consistency in behaviour, and an emotional pact in which the party doing the trusting invests some personal commitment in the other. Underpinning trust is integrity. Integrity is values-driven behaviour, behaviour that is driven by a clear and coherent set of ethical standards, producing consistency and making it possible for past performance to be used as an indicator of future behaviour. However, trust in business and, more significantly, in business leaders has sunk to an all time low, as these examples illustrate.

Enron

Enron used some highly dubious methods to ensure that its high risk business activity was laundered through off-balance sheet 'partnerships' which enabled the company to appear financially sound, giving it access to stock market funds and low interest credit (lower risk improves a company's credit rating and, therefore, the availability and price of loans). After several years' fame as the darling of the markets, it achieved notoriety as the USA's largest ever bankruptcy.

WorldCom

WorldCom was built, through acquisitions, into a major telecoms business and the second largest long distance supplier of telecoms services after AT&T, and also became a darling of the stock market as its rapid growth and profitability pushed its share price ever skywards. However, the WorldCom bubble burst when the company was forced to restate its profits and it became apparent that it had disguised expenditure as capital investment and treated loans as revenue, to inflate its profits.

Global Crossing

Global Crossing was another telecoms business, this time a company specialising in laying the fibre optic cables that carry voice and data signals around the world. As the Internet grew exponentially during the early nineties, and as demand for bandwidth (the capacity of telecoms cables to carry those signals) grew, companies vied with each other to lay longer, fatter cables. As its name suggests, Global Crossing laid cables round the world. Unfortunately, so did many other companies. The days when forecasters suggested that the information society would run out of capacity to keep itself informed has given way to suggestions that much of this optical fibre will remain dark, never used to carry anything. Over-capacity leads, of course, to collapsing prices. And companies that have borrowed heavily to invest find that they just don't have the revenue to keep going. In 1997 Global Crossing was valued at $55bn, even more than General Motors; by 2002 it declared bankruptcy owing $12bn, which really takes some doing!

Equitable Life

Equitable Life was one of the UK's leading insurance and pension companies, a mutual organisation, whose customers also owned the business. It had a reputation for offering above average returns, which it traded on to attract new customers. Its downfall arose because it offered guarantees to some of its customers that their pension funds would achieve levels that, in the late eighties and early nineties, were easily attainable. Unfortunately, the low inflation nineties caused investment income to fall and Equitable Life tried to avoid its guarantees by reducing other parts of the payout to maturing policies. This, the House of Lords decided, was a breach of the original contract with savers, and Equitable Life was forced almost into bankruptcy, cutting drastically the value of policies and ruining the retirement plans of thousands of people.

Marconi

Marconi, the last of this elite group, didn't start out with that name. For over 30 years Arnold Weinstock had built the company, called GEC, into the UK's most successful engineering business, producing everything from toasters to warships. Weinstock kept a tight rein on the businesses that made up the GEC conglomerate, and was heavily criticised in the city for being unadventurous. What that seemed to mean was that he had over £1bn in cash in the bank and didn't engage in protracted takeover battles. City financial institutions make their profits by lending money and advising on takeovers so GEC didn't need their services very much, but when Weinstock left, the new managers went on a spree, selling off 'old economy' businesses and reinventing the company as – wait for it – another telecoms business! Marconi wanted to be up there with the big boys, like Lucent and Cisco, making the clever electronics that enabled the world's information systems to work. Instead, it finished up as a basket case, with so much debt that it narrowly escaped bankruptcy.

Ethics, trust and leadership

So what have all these companies got in common, apart from either going bankrupt of narrowly escaping it? The answer is, they each had a dominant figure, one widely respected (or, at least, treated with great respect by those he came into contact with, which may not be exactly the same thing), who led them up the hill to initial success, and then part way down again into the depths, before leaving with a pay off which seemed to reward failure. The reality of these figures, now that the truth is beginning to appear, is that they mixed enormous personal authority with a deep sense of self worth – they appear to have believed that they could do no wrong, even when they were making decisions that, in the cold light of day, ranged from the extremely reckless to (in some cases it has been alleged), fraudulent.

Asset-lite or ethics-lite?

At Enron, Chairman and Chief Executive Kenneth Lay, assisted by ideas man Jeffrey Shilling, who briefly succeeded his boss after the business went into financial meltdown, created what Peter Fusaro and Ross Miller (authors of *'What went wrong at Enron'*) called an 'asset-lite' company. The energy business was big business, usually involving large amounts of capital tied up in exploration, generation or storage. What Enron did was to expand not just its operations in the utilities industry (it bought Wessex Water in the UK, for example) but also acted as a market maker – buying and selling energy as intermediary between producers and users. Such intermediaries use

59

the price mechanism to control both sides of the market, making a profit on the margins between the two, a profit that is related in part to the risk they take in taking positions (setting prices and buying or selling volumes which they may or may not actually have at the time).

But Enron didn't stop at gas or oil – it also set up markets in pollution rights, paper pulp and speciality chemicals. They even got involved in swap and option contracts based on the weather to provide a hedge against sharp changes that might affect agriculture or demands for power.

One problem with this twin track strategy was that expanding production capability demands high levels of investment which increase debt, whereas acting as a market maker means having high levels of credit to give trading partners confidence in Enron's ability to meet their commitments. It was this conflict that led to the creation of apparently independent entities, through which debt was hidden, in order to ensure that the balance sheet looked healthy, keeping the company's credit rating high.

A company's balance sheet, along with its profit and loss account, is a primary record of the company's financial status. It shows what the company owns (its assets) and what it owes (its liabilities). Unfortunately, whether or not an asset or liability appears on a company's balance sheet is largely a matter of choice. For example, a company may choose to buy new equipment through bank borrowing. This creates a liability and adds to its assets. Alternatively, the asset could be leased for a fixed period, and so not appear on the balance sheet at all, as it remains the property of the finance company. Why does this matter? It matters because the scale of bank lending relative to the money invested by shareholders (equity capital) is regarded as a key measure of risk. This quotient of equity to loan capital, namely, the gearing ratio, indicates how risk is being shared between the owners and the company's creditors.

What Enron did was more sophisticated than simply lease assets. It was engaged in complicated financial transactions, buying and selling energy (gas, oil, electricity) to balance supply and demand between producers and consumers (or, to be more precise suppliers to domestic and commercial users). This is a high-risk enterprise, as 'promises' of future supplies are bought and sold, with the intermediary taking a profit on the difference between the prices as a reward for shouldering the risk.

Much of this trading is done by initially paying only a small part of the value of the trade, so that the capital tied up in the options (to buy or sell at a fixed price) is only a fraction of the true liability or asset acquired. What's more, the profitability of the trades tends to be directly related to the risk, so the largest profits go to those who take the greatest risks – as do the greatest potential losses. What Enron did was to create separate companies through which the highest risk trades were placed. By injecting small amounts of capital, large risks could be taken which weren't reflected in Enron's own accounts.

Self-belief or self-delusion

The huge upswing in the financial markets and its subsequent collapse in the late nineties is often thought to be due to the dot.com boom – the vast amounts of money sucked in by and then written off by businesses that were going to be the next Amazon (itself only just breaking even after all these years). But, according to Keith Brody and Sancha Dunstan (in *'The Great Telecoms Swindle'*) the real culprits were the telecoms businesses. From vastly over-paying for licences for the third generation of mobile phones just coming onto an already mature market to paying over-the-top prices for businesses in a takeover mania, telecoms companies seemed to lose control of common sense in a market that would need to keep growing exponentially to justify their rash investment. Why? What was wrong at these companies that made them seem lose all sense of reason and moral responsibility for the long term welfare of their businesses, its employees and shareholders?

At WorldCom, the reason was Bernie Ebbers, at Global Crossing it was Gary Winnick, and at Marconi it was George Simpson. These three CEOs, like Lay (and Shilling) at Enron, seemed to have such a self-belief and lust for excitement that keeping their businesses in a constant fever of expansion, takeover and change seemed like an end in itself. However, their headlong rush into growth at almost any price was aided and abetted by some fundamental weaknesses in both the system of corporate governance that failed to restrain them and in the financial institutions that encouraged and served them.

John Plender (in *'Going off the Rails'*) argues very cogently that corporate governance in the Anglo-Saxon market capitalism world failed to restrain CEOs like these due to systemic weaknesses. He argues that the emphasis on shareholder value – basically, the need to ensure an increasing return to investors – has led to a dangerously short-term attitude in which growth and profits become an end in themselves, rather than a basis for creating a sustainable long-term business. This is coupled with over-generous reward systems for CEOs only loosely connected to performance (measured, of course, in terms of share prices and profits) and short periods in the job, with most lasting less than four years.

So who can you trust?

Carly Fiorina, then Chief Executive and Chairman of Hewlett-Packard, speaking at the CBI conference in November 2002, said that *'The reputation of business as a whole has been badly damaged (by scandals like Enron and WorldCom) and it is business leaders who are in a unique position to restore faith in free enterprise. The lessons to be learned are starkly simple. What was behind the fraudulent mismanagement of the disgraced companies comes down to greed, pure and simple, coupled with the belief that the stakeholders – employees, customers, investors and the communities in which the businesses operate – could be deceived.'*

Although managers of these businesses were under pressure to deliver 'optimistic results', Fiorina argued that it was still greed that underpinned the unrealistic expectations of the financial market for fat shareholder dividends. *'Businesses which cave in to that pressure do so to the long-term detriment of the business.'*

The financial services industry also has a vested interest in encouraging takeovers and creative financial management. The big investment banks made money out of Marconi by advising it on selling off parts of the business, on acquiring new businesses, on borrowing money to fund this, and then on settling with its creditors when its finances ran into problems. This could be justified as simply providing a service that was needed, but some of the practices of these investment banks seemed deliberately to mislead the public. For example, the New York Attorney-General recently agreed a $150m fine with Credit Suisse First Boston for its practice of pushing new share offers (the Initial Public Offerings or IPOs that launched so many failed new technology businesses) whilst, at the same time, its own analysts were rubbishing them.

And the people we should be able to rely on don't seem quite so reliable any more. Arthur Anderson, the now extinct auditors at Enron and WorldCom, earned more money from consultancy (four times as much at WorldCom) as they did from auditing. What auditor is going to say that the company's finances are dodgy when it is earning money helping the company to engage in exactly the practices which cause the concern – and when most of the top financial team at the company are ex-colleagues (as they were at Enron)? Whilst most people assume that auditors are simply applying standard accounting rules to judge the company's financial status, as an article in the *Harvard Business Review* ('Why Good Accountants Do Bad Audits' HBR Nov. 2002 pp. 97-102) pointed out *'the real problem isn't conscious corruption, it's unconscious bias'*. The combination of the subjective nature of accounting (a fact many people would be surprised about) and the close relationship with clients makes it hard for auditors to uncover or recognise malpractice.

Should we blame it on the system?
Unfortunately, as Plender explains, the alternatives to market capitalism are even more problematic. In Asia, the 'crony capitalism' of cross-holdings between banks and their customers and between customers and suppliers, and the strong links between government and business means that decision-making can be even more flawed. Problems, once they occur, can bring down the whole pack of cards. One failure in the network of relationships can precipitate failure for all.

In continental Europe, the stakeholder system, whereby most finance is supplied by bank lending, and where those banks then have their own representatives sitting on supervisory boards alongside representatives of the employees, discourages innovation and change.

The flexibility of the labour markets in the US and UK may mean that individuals suffer, but it also encourages new businesses to start up and investment in higher risk businesses. The failures in the telecoms infrastructure industry are predominately in the UK and US because that's where the industry grew most rapidly.

But at Equitable Life many of these characteristics were absent. There were no investment bankers encouraging headlong spending sprees on takeovers, and the need to ensure that shareholders got growth in their share prices and larger and larger dividends wasn't there because there were no shareholders to satisfy. So what made Equitable Life go off the rails? Again it seems that Equitable's CEOs, first Roy Ranson and then his protégé Alan Nash (who was also Equitable's Actuary – the professional responsible for assessing risk) had been bitten by the same bug of self-belief and reluctance to listen to doubters. They embarked on a major campaign of expansion to make Equitable a major player in the industry, not just by giving unrealistic guarantees to policy-holders but, as a recent report has discovered, by paying out bonuses to policy-holders that weren't justified by the returns being earned.

Such a strategy reeks of the same attitude that wrecked Marconi, WorldCom and Global Crossing, that growth is an end in itself and that the market will keep on growing because it has to, to justify the strategies being pursued. This is not what leadership is about. Good leadership, strong leadership, effective leadership, call it what you will, leadership is not about over-confidence and demanding blind loyalty, which seemed to be a common feature of these organisations' bosses.

This sort of strategy also betrays an attitude to ethics in decision-making that assumes any behaviour is permissible if it leads to the desired outcomes. This contrasts with the belief that our behaviour should be driven by moral values, and not just the outcomes; in other words, we are contrasting belief in 'the ends justify the means' versus a belief that the means themselves must be morally justifiable. The consequentialist approach ('the ends justify the means'), which is what moral philosophers call it, is summed up in the quote by Gordon Gekko (played by Michael Douglas) in the film Wall Street: *'Greed is good'*

Why is greed good? Because in the extreme view of capitalism held by his character (and by many of the executives referred to here), by always aiming to maximise your own economic welfare, you raise the economic welfare of all. This belief was supported by the 'trickle down' theory, that if the rich get richer the poor will also get richer, because wealth trickles down in their expenditure. However, the collapse of stock markets in the 1990s showed that it was pensioners and endowment policy owners who paid the price of the optimistic investment bankers' foolishness, whereas many of them lost little or nothing.

By contrast, people prefer leaders who exhibit clear values and beliefs in their actions, and are willing to be judged by their behaviour rather than their effects. This is what philosophers since Plato have been discussing when they talked about moral character. For them, a good moral character was one whose actions were, regularly and reliably, appropriate and reasonable. Of course, what is appropriate and reasonable leads into a debate about the values that guide our behaviour, but what dominates is the emphasis on the behaviour itself demonstrating being values-driven.

Leadership also involves being open to questioning and challenge from others and from yourself, without being plagued by them. Leadership means recognising that the world is an uncertain place and that confidence comes from being aware of the risks and allowing for them, not ignoring them. A good leader takes a compass and map, but also takes a survival kit just in case – and makes sure that the rest of the party has one too.

That's not to say that leadership is about caution, quite the reverse. Good leaders take risks because they understand the risk and have allowed for it in their plans. After all, as TS Eliot wrote, *'Only those who will risk going too far can possibly find out how far one can go'*. Unfortunately, poor leaders – and that's what all these organisations suffered from – treat risks as something that only lesser mortals fear and kept going heedlessly, but then caused those same lesser mortals (their employees and shareholders) to pay the price of their lack of caution.

People trust leaders who take risks if they show, by word and deed, that the risks have been assessed and that the path being followed is the right one. Most importantly of all, that those leaders share the risks that others are being asked to take and aren't cocooned in share options, pension rights and employment contracts that ensure that no matter what happens, they won't suffer as those they lead may have to suffer. Trust comes not from always being right, but by showing that your self-belief is tempered by an appreciation of the implications of your actions on others and a willingness not to ask anyone to do something that you wouldn't do yourself. In other words, from the practices and understanding that comes from a high EQ – being self-aware and being aware of others' emotional states. Recognising the difference between what you want to happen to make your plans come true, and what is really happening. The analytical decision-making that is assumed to be the hallmark of effective leaders at the top of giant corporations needs an understanding and recognition of the emotions that can sway decision unless they are acknowledged and accounted for.

Putting the boot into corporate greed

Surveys by Penna, the HR consultancy, and by Exploratum market research found that many employees are bored with their work and have a dim view of the leadership qualities of their company's managers. 'More confidence in using soft skills to gain hard benefits' was cited by David Fairhurst as a key necessity for store directors and managers in Tesco, one of the top companies that were employers of choice. An emphasis on the need for middle managers' leadership ability was noted by McCarthy of Penna, rather than a focus on the media driven 'superhero' charismatic senior leader.

Making workers proud of the firm is not however the whole story; commercial success allied with happy staff is the combination that any success seeking enterprise is likely to aspire to. Research also shows that investors believe socially responsible companies deliver better returns on investment, while employees cite a company's set of values as a key factor in determining their place of employment.

While companies like Virgin, Amazon and Microsoft were listed as employers of choice in the Penna and Exploratum reports, we have chosen the Timberland Corporation as one of our 'cameos' of a classic tale of EQ in practice because of its focus on both happy staff and corporate social responsibility. Timberland was founded in 1918 as a small company in southeast Boston by Nathan Swartz, grandfather of Jeff Swartz the current CEO, with an emphasis from the start on caring for its employees as a core company value. Angela Jameson (writing in The Times business section in May 2004) reports Swartz recalling his father telling him as a small boy 'We have to take care of each other', after inadvertently witnessing the giving of extra money to one of his workers in need.

His grandfather's ability to understand others and the challenges they face has remained a company value with a pay off in long term corporate achievements. Corporate social responsibility remains a core value of Timberland with today's company philosophy integrating investment in the community with an aim to be free of toxins, carbon neutral and using 100% renewable resources as key to the company's strategic direction. The evidence of applied EQ and how this contributes to peoples' motivation is aptly demonstrated by Timberland's workforce putting in 270,000 hours of volunteer time in 2003 to company supported community initiatives. Even when the company was almost bankrupted in 1994, Timberland's defence of community policy paid off in the long term with the loyalty shown by its staff and customers to achieve current annual revenues of $1.3 billion (£700 million) and $31 million in profits in the first quarter of 2004.

> The EQ emphasis on awareness of others and an ethical framework of principles and values are fundamental to Timberland Corporation's approach. This was effectively endorsed by Jeff Swartz in his keynote speech 'Uniting value and values for business success', at the Ethical Corp Europe 2004 conference.
>
> Further information is available on:
>
> **http://www.ethicalcorp.com/europe2004/printprogramme.shtml**
>
> **http://greatplacetowork.co.uk/best/list-bestusa-2004.htm**
>
> **http://www.timberland.com/timberlandserve/timberlandserve_index.jsp**

Trust from within, trust from without

But trust needs to exist within organisations as well. A report by Dr Carsten Sørensen of the London School of Economics and Political Science, commissioned by Microsoft and entitled *The Future Role of Trust in Work* looked at the growing number of organisations employing highly skilled and qualified people, what he calls information workers. He comments that *'Lack of mutual trust can lead to severe consequences for all... If employees perceive that they are being watched too closely or that the information being collected is not being used appropriately, they will find ways round monitoring.'* Furthermore, he argues, *'the issue of trust cuts both ways. Management must relinquish some of the control of direct observation'.*

Research published in early 2001 by the IABC Research Foundation for United Technologies (*'Measuring Organisational Trust: A Diagnostic Survey and International Indicator'*) emphasised the importance of trust for profitability and innovation. They argued that, because it is based on different values for each individual, organisational trust is not a simple or unified concept. The research identified the multiple factors that shape trust, and grouped them into five dimensions:

- competence (employees' and leaders' effectiveness)
- openness and honesty (amount, accuracy and sincerity of information shared)
- concern for employees (exhibition of empathy, tolerance and safety)
- reliability (consistent and dependable actions)
- identification (sharing common goals, values and beliefs)

As these five dimensions create organisational trust – trust in turn proves to have a statistically significant relationship in creating job satisfaction and perceived organisational effectiveness. In addition, the research suggests that organisations with high levels of trust benefit from more adaptive organisational structures and more responsive virtual teams. This link between trust and the ability to cope with the unexpected and to innovate makes organisations that are more likely to survive in the increasingly uncertain world of the 21st century.

One finding from the IABC research was that trust helps organisations operate globally. Global business has not had a good press, attracting large-scale demonstrations to World Trade Organisation meetings in Seattle, for example. One of the major objections to global companies is their search for ever-cheaper sources of supplies, especially in the textiles and shoe industry. Companies like Gap, Old Navy and Nike have been accused of exploitation and connivance with autocratic governments in developing countries to support their own profits. What really unites anti-globalisation protesters is a belief that globalisation is underpinned by unethical behaviour. For some, that simply means capitalism, and it's probable that no argument could be made that would be acceptable to them. For others, the case is more complex. It's not so much capitalism that they oppose, but its raw, uncontrolled and excessive power, as expressed by large, global companies. In particular, the power such companies have seemingly to over-ride local opinion and political processes.

In other words, their opposition is selective. They object to the use of untried technologies like GM foods, which they believe threaten indigenous species. They object to the political patronage (and even corruption) that such companies support. Companies like Esso have attracted criticism for their financial support of politicians and parties in pursuit of a favourable climate for their corporate goals and it has even spawned its own specific opposition, the StopEsso campaign, opposing its refusal to acknowledge the impact of hydrocarbon fuels on the global climate. Their opponents simply do not trust them.

Trust depends on leadership

And for trust to exist, an organisation needs effective leaders. OPP Ltd are employee selection and development specialists. They commissioned a survey in July 2000 to find out what people thought of the people who lead their organisations. The 1,000 respondents represented a broad cross-section of the working population, and their views showed a depressing lack of trust in their leaders and a mismatch between what they are looking for in the way of leadership, and what they are actually getting.

According to Dr Robert McHenry, founder and chairman of OPP

'Due to the poor quality of leadership and management in this country, the workforce is confused with regard to the needs of the company over the employee's own needs. This confusion results in lack of motivation, direction and desire for the company to succeed, and with it go the fortunes of employees and shareholders......some of the best (leaders) convey clarity of direction and reassure individuals that they are safe and secure; some of the worst include pushing too hard and creating uncertainty and fear.'

Clearly, leaders in the UK are facing new challenges as organisations evolve faster than ever. This report suggested that many leaders are failing under the pressure; just four people in ten were satisfied with the quality of leadership in their organisation, while only a quarter believed that leadership in the UK had improved over the previous ten years.

What is most interesting is that leaders who were entrepreneurial and risk taking are the least popular among UK employees, reflecting a move towards more 'safe leadership' in today's volatile business climate. At the heart of the problem was the failure of leaders to live up to employees' expectations. The majority of respondents believed trust was the most essential leadership quality, yet less than a quarter regarded this as their boss's greatest attribute. Such gaps between reality and expectation create dissatisfaction among workers, who want leaders with good people skills rather than the more traditional 'command and control' style of leadership.

The importance of trust, revealed by the research was significant – 69% of respondents believing this to be an absolutely essential quality. Hampered by a lack of trust, many UK leaders fail to live up to employees' expectations, explaining perhaps why only four in ten respondents were satisfied with the quality of leadership in their organisations. There was a clear mismatch between employees' expectations of leadership and what they actually experienced, leading to widespread dissatisfaction in the workplace. Again, according to Robert McHenry: *'It is becoming harder to trust leaders... as it is rare to find any leader who is prepared to be open and honest. There are too many hidden agendas.'*

Other qualities, such as being a good communicator, decisive and motivational also featured highly, suggesting employees value bosses with good people skills. Meanwhile, qualities traditionally associated with people who lead organisations – being visionary, strategic and drivers of change – were considered less important. Being entrepreneurial or a risk-taker ranked bottom of a list of twelve qualities, suggesting employees crave 'safe leadership', i.e. leaders who make them feel included and cared for.

'How important are the following leadership qualities?'

Leadership Quality	Absolutely essential
Trust	69%
Good communicator	64%
Decisive	54%
Motivational	47%

Inspirational	40%
People focused	36%
Visionary	28%
Strategic	25%
Driver of change	17%
Charismatic	16%
Entrepreneurial	9%
A risk taker	7%

Source: OPP

A lack of trust inside organisations means that people waste time proving that they are being productive instead of actually being effective. As the old saying about quality management goes, 'you don't fatten a pig by weighing it'. A lack of trust outside organisations, trust by customers, shareholders or the wider community means that they are reluctant to make any emotional investment in the organisation. Customers have no loyalty, shareholders want bigger and bigger returns now because they have no faith in promises of future returns, and the community at large is cynical about any decision made by organisations that may affect them or those that they identify with.

Research by the Gallup Organisation in 2001 found that conventional measures of customer satisfaction are inadequate in establishing the true level of trust felt by customers and others. The measures they have developed show that there are often enormous variations between people's ratings of their satisfaction with a good or poor service and their true feelings about the organisation. Organisations need to recognise that just because customers are reasonably happy with the last transaction it doesn't mean that they necessarily have any real emotional attachment to it. They will happily change suppliers because their brand preference does not imply that they have any real loyalty. Loyalty has to be earned by more than simply offering adequate levels of service or competitive prices. Gallup uses customers' sense of confidence, integrity, pride and passion in an organisation as the basis for their measure of this emotional attachment.

If they are to generate trust, the senior managers of organisations need to be aware that they are engaged in an emotional relationship with others. In practice, this means that managers and leaders at all levels need to be alert to their personal responsibility for engendering trust. This starts with self-awareness and understanding of their own feelings and the signals being sent. Is the behaviour which is intended to generate trust a true reflection of what individuals really feel, as opposed to what they think they ought to feel? Trust also means being aware of others, recognising, acknowledging and understanding the legitimacy of others' feelings. When organisations' spokespeople deride their critics for being emotional or irrational in their views, they are exposing their own emotional illiteracy, because all they are doing is reinforcing negative perceptions.

Ultimately, trust depends on the organisation's behaviour being driven by an ethical framework of principles and values, by an awareness of the overall situation, the emotions shaping attitudes and behaviour, and by open and honest communication. People will be more trusting of the organisation or person promising little and delivering all that is promised, than the one promising the earth and merely delivering a continent! The true arbiter of trust is performance and the match that exists between performance and what was promised or expected. Building trust requires that leaders and managers of organisations develop their self-awareness and their awareness of others' emotions, and are able to reflect on this and use this reflection to shape their behaviour. By contrast, losing trust is easy; it just takes one wrong word or one wrong deed. Just ask Gerald Ratner!

Creativity, innovation and EQ

If trust reflects the level of 'corporate' EQ (or at least, the level of EQ within senior decision-makers) then so does creativity and innovation. This may come as a surprise, since creativity and innovation are rarely discussed in the same breath as emotional intelligence, but the ability of an organisation to encourage creativity in its workforce and to encourage innovation in its processes and its products and services, is very much a function of leadership EQ.

It's almost too obvious to point out that we live in a rapidly increasing world of change, but it needs emphasising because the rate of change is critical to organisational performance. Today, organisations either lead change and shape the world they operate in, or they follow behind, desperately adapting to the world that others have made. Two quotes on change we like especially:

'It is not the strongest of the species that survive, nor the most intelligent, but the one most responsive to change.'
Charles Darwin

'Progress is impossible without change, and those who cannot change their minds cannot change anything.'
George Bernard Shaw

Niccolò Machiavelli also pointed out the personal challenge that is involved in leading change, when he suggested *'There is nothing more difficult to take in hand, more perilous to conduct, or more uncertain in its success than to take the lead in the introduction of a new order of things.'*

It's also worth remembering that the first telephone was introduced in Britain in the late 1870s and it took the next hundred years for one half of all households to have a telephone. It only took just over 20 years, from the late 1970s to the year 2000, for more or less the whole population to have a phone at home – that's a doubling of the level of ownership in one fifth of the time. By comparison, 1985 saw the launch of the first mobile phone service in the UK. By 2002, 91% of households had at least one mobile phone. In 17 years, the proportion of homes having at least one mobile phone reached the level that it took landlines over a century to reach.

Why does this matter? Because these figures reflect the enormous changes that have taken place in the way we live and the jobs we do. Call centres hardly existed until the 1980s. What was the point when so few people had phones? Now, they are one of the most common types of job. The existence of call centres depends upon there being a level of phone ownership and usage to make it viable to offer it as the primary means of contact with an organisation and one that will be accepted (albeit reluctantly in many cases) by consumers.

The effect of technological and social change combines to change the kind of jobs people have the way that they are managed and led. Just recently, one of the writers met someone whose job involves identifying possible tunes to use as mobile phone ring tones and making them available over the Internet. Ten years ago, mobile phones all used standard ring tones and the Internet barely existed, so his job could not even be envisaged, let alone performed. Now it is possible to describe it easily and simply, as it reflects a reality that we all recognise. And just as some jobs and some organisations appear as a result of technological and social changes, others disappear. In this process, people feel substantial dislocation and fear; fear of the new and fear of what is being lost. Again, managers and leaders have to help people cope with this.

A key feature of the rapid rate of change is people's response to innovative products, services and work patterns. As we saw earlier, some people are more predisposed towards innovation, those with a high 'O' Factor (openness to new ideas), which is reflected in their enthusiasm for novelty. But new products, services and work processes don't appear out of thin air. They have to be created, and it is the ability of organisations to encourage and harness the creativity of the people they employ that will determine if they are able to lead change through their innovative abilities, or follow behind. It is not enough for organisation to talk creativity and innovation; they have to walk the talk.

The corporate criteria for innovation

One company that has earned a serious reputation as an innovator and which describes itself largely in terms of its ability to innovate, is 3M. Bill Coyne, who was at that time the Senior Vice-President, R&D for the 3M Corporation, gave the sixth UK Innovation Lecture at the Queen Elizabeth 11 Conference Centre on the 5th March 1996. In it he described creativity as the *'thinking of novel and appropriate ideas'* and innovation as *'the successful implementation of those ideas within an organisation'*. This is a useful distinction, between cause (creativity) and effect (innovation). Organisations that seek to be innovative need to attract, support and encourage creativity in the people they employ, and ensure that the ideas creativity generates get translated into innovative processes, products and services.

The Centre for Exploitation of Science and Technology (CEST) call this the 'Innovation Gap', the gap between vision and reality, between the idea generation and analysis which identifies the potential of a new idea or process (Coyne's creativity) and its implementation, from foresight to wealth creation. 3M have a similar concept which they label 'white space'; this is the gap between existing products and the identified market need. An organisation needs to have mechanisms for identifying and occupying the white space.

Bill Coyne identified six characteristics of 3M which, he suggests have enabled the company to be regarded as innovatory, despite their size and age as a corporation. These characteristics are:

- vision
- foresight
- stretch goals
- empowerment
- communication
- rewards and recognition.

Vision is not just a sense of purpose but a purpose which explicitly includes innovation and one which is constantly translated into practice by employees. Vision is where we want to go.

Foresight is the ability to predict accurately where customers are going, how they will react to the changing environment in which they live. It involves identifying their needs, both the articulated need, reflecting problems which customers are aware of (e.g., to replace CFC as a propellant in aerosols), and unarticulated needs, those requiring a real insight into the customers' situation.

The best illustration of this is the need for masking tape seen by

3M's Dick Drew in 1923. Drew was a specialist in sandpaper and was exploring what was the best material to be used by sprayers repainting vehicles. At the time, two-tone cars were becoming popular and people were having their cars painted, and sprayers were using tape to mask off the area not being painted. Unfortunately, the tape tended to damage the paint and so they had to clean off the area using fine sandpaper and touch it up by hand. Drew recognised that the solution to their problem was not better abrasives but a tape that didn't damage the surface. So masking tape was invented.

Another example of this ability to recognise the unarticulated need was another 3M creative genius, Art Fry. It was his idea to put low-adhesive glue on notelets which produced Post-it™ notes. Vision and foresight help to set a culture of innovation, but people need to be pushed to go beyond simple incremental improvements. 3M's stretch goals include:

- 30% of sales to be from products introduced in last 4 years
- 10% of sales to be from products introduced in last year

This creates a sense of urgency; innovation is time sensitive, missing market opportunities can seriously reduce profitability. This is more than empty rhetoric, it means giving people some say over how they use their time. At 3M, technical staff have the right to spend up to 15% of their time on projects of their own choosing. Their project outcomes are not measured, but giving this freedom is a notional concept which creates a climate in which an individual's initiative is positively expected – a form of institutionalised revolution! For every 1,000 ideas, only 100 become formal proposals, and only a few of these become new product ventures – of which over half fail. For 3M, working to these ratios is essential for them to remain at the leading edge in their various markets.

The idea of project choice means creating an open organisation in which easy communication and networking is possible, enabling multi-disciplinary teams to be created and the cross-fertilisation of ideas to occur. Many new ideas involve the application of existing technologies to new product areas (e.g. of micro-replication from optical to mechanical and then to electronic applications). This communication is based on three ground rules:

a. products belong to divisions but technologies belong to the company
b. multiple methods for sharing information, including technical fairs and forums managed by the technical staff, plus technical audits to identify technology transfer possibilities
c. staff are told that networking is their responsibility, and communication systems and the 15% rule facilitate that process.

3M has special award programmes for recognising innovation, often based on peer recognition, and offers promotion on a dual ladder to either advanced technical grades or to management posts so that creative people don't have to give up their work in order to gain advancement. However, there is no direct financial reward for specific innovations – it's considered that it's their job to innovate!

These characteristics are not sufficient for innovation to occur, but they have been necessary in 3M's case and allowed it to remain a leading player in a wide range of rapidly changing markets. In fact, if they can't be at the leading edge they will spin off the products, as they need the high value, high margin business that comes from being early into the market to sustain their R&D base.

But you can't make people think creatively – what's needed is an environment in which creative thinking is welcomed and nurtured. Creativity is all about novelty and breaking down existing ways of thinking and doing. The rational, logical, scientific way of addressing problems has its strengths, but it also has its weaknesses. It encourages a narrow, one-track approach that can become limiting by excluding ways of thinking that break through those conventional boundaries. That's why 3M have seen the need to encourage creativity as requiring systems and structures in place, not simply as rhetoric.

Creating the emotional climate for innovation

So, what has this to do with emotional intelligence? Everything! Thinking creatively requires an environment in which novelty is valued and fostered, not one where it is scorned or discouraged. Managers and leaders need to be alert to originality and creativity wherever it comes from, and ensure that their reactions to new ideas, however outlandish or off the wall they may appear, encourage people to think what Coyne called 'novel and appropriate ideas'.

Research by PA Management Consultants in the 1970s suggested that organisational resistance to innovation can become endemic, characterised by 'one-correct answer' thinking and failures to challenge the obvious ('it ain't broke so don't fix it'), coupled with negativity ('we tried that once and it didn't work') and pressures to conform (the 'not invented here' syndrome). Above all there is often a fear of looking foolish by challenging the accepted wisdom or, even worse, trying something new and failing.

Novelty is often problematic. New ideas don't work well at first. James Dyson took 5 years and 5,127 prototypes before the world's first bagless vacuum cleaner arrived. As Francis Bacon said, in 1625:

'As the births of all living creatures are, at first, misshapen, so are all innovations ...'

The leaders and managers in organisations set the tone of the organisation in its openness to creativity and innovation, by their own behaviour in response to the ideas that are presented to them and by the way that the organisation is structured and operates. This is often described in terms of its culture. In *'The Change Masters'* Rosabeth Moss Kanter described many organisations as being highly segmental, where self-contained units compartmentalise problems and solutions, with strong ownership and boundaries reinforced by high power structures. This is contrasted with what she calls 'integrative action' organisations, where problems are approached as wholes, attached to larger wholes, for which new connections can be sought, with low power structures. This is the structure that 3M has endeavoured to create.

Let emotional intelligence thrive

We are not arguing that creativity and innovation require emotionally intelligent organisations, because emotional intelligence is a personal quality and not something that is possessed by the organisation itself, but by the people that make it up. (Of course, you could argue that organisations are no more than the people they employ, which is largely true, but as people change so the organisation changes and it is the people we want to concentrate on.) What we are saying is that creativity and innovation can only blossom fully where emotionally intelligent people work. They need to recognise the effect that their attitudes and behaviour can have on each other.

It is too easy for people to dampen enthusiasm for new ideas by their lack of commitment to the organisation or their colleagues, by their cynicism and general negativity. It's far too easy to respond to suggestions for new ways of working or new products or services by identifying the barriers to their introduction, to explain why they won't work. All too often this is not a rational response identifying real difficulties, but an emotional response revealing our own fears of the unknown, of risk, of uncertainty. Emotionally intelligent leaders can recognise this and use this knowledge to overcome their own resistance to new ideas, understand the real reasons for others' resistance and develop solutions that acknowledge and don't ignore these emotional responses of others.

The biggest problem faced by most organisations, given the ever-increasing rate of change, is however the uncertainty and confusion that they are presented with. Old certainties are wiped away by changing technology, behaviour and expectations. Chuck Palus and David Horth's book *'The Leader's Edge'* argues that when we encounter confusion, our natural instinct is to try and make order from it – generally by looking for the things that we recognise that explain the situation and enable us to resolve any problems that have been generated. This tendency, which they call sense-making, combines our analytical, logical and intuitive abilities – after all, one of the most remarkable things about humans is the gift we have to see patterns in the most confused or partial data. Yet this gift is also a curse. The patterns we look for and see are the patterns that are familiar, expected or predicted. This is where the technical strength of managers can become a weakness – they look for the things they will recognise, and see patterns that fit with their expectations. But complexity often doesn't present expected or predictable patterns, and the ability to see patterns can become a desire to impose patterns on these complex challenges.

This complexity is increasing as markets become more global, as the pace of technological development increases, and as the effects of competitive forces (in all sectors, not just the private sector) make it imperative to get new products and services to market quicker and maintain pace with the changes in other organisations. Sense-making can easily become sense-forcing – and the consequences can be disastrous, if the sense that is made is wrong. From Nick Leeson at Barings to the catastrophic decline of Marconi, the wrong decisions were made by people who honestly believed that they understood what was happening and that, by continuing with a strategy which was demonstrably failing, they were going to make good.

Chuck Palus and David Horth identify creativity as being a key dimension of leadership, and emphasise the various skills that are needed to make the model work, and the need to develop these skills by a structured and long-term development programme. They also emphasise the importance of organisational development alongside leadership development. As Chuck Palus says:

'These (creative) competencies have two aspects – they are held and practised by individuals, and, they are also held and practised at the organisational level as part of culture, values, and shared practice. It is especially when the latter aspect is realised that an organisation has what we call connected leadership.'

For organisations to foster creativity and innovation, they need to encourage people to be self-aware, to understand their own emotions, listen to and reflect on their intuitive feelings when faced with ideas and concepts that challenge their preconceived notions of how things should be done. They should avoid immediate responses, and discourage others from responding quickly, and instead think about how they feel about the idea – and why. They also need to recognise their own body language signals and associated emotions, and

81

consider what messages they send out when something new and challenging is discussed.

Similarly, they need to be interested in and aware of others' body language and behaviours, and interpret and anticipate others' emotions when presented with something novel and unfamiliar. How do people react – and why? They need to be able to reflect on creative ideas and suggestions for innovative processes, products and services, not respond immediately with a purely emotional reaction.

Reflection means placing the idea within an ethical framework of principles and values, to take a broad overview of the situation, to think about their own emotions and others' anticipated emotions, and to be prepared to communicate openly and honestly with all those involved. Only when they have reflected on the ideas and suggestions should people respond, using behaviour that reflects recognition of their own and others' emotions and in a way that matches their ethical principles and values. Although seemingly simple, the application of **EQ4U** can enable organisations to foster the creativity and innovation that all organisations need if they are to prosper and develop in the 21st century.

The leadership challenge

'The supreme quality for a leader is unquestionably integrity.'
Dwight D Eisenhower

How do leaders respond to these challenges? At a global level, the accelerating pace of change and increasing international interdependence emphasises the importance of effective relationships and strategic partnerships between world leaders. Increasing international perspectives and awareness of global causes and effects on politics, business and society mean a greater need for interdependent leadership approaches and effective international relationships, with a common set of core values and principles at its heart. Colin Powell's (2003) personal integrity-based assertion that the USA's National Security Strategy focuses above all on alliances and partnerships and puts a priority on developing strong co-operative relations with other major powers is testament to this approach.

Within this wider context, we expect political and religious leaders to demonstrate applied integrity in both their professional and personal lives. In the same way, business leaders are expected to behave in a way that engenders confidence in their ability to deliver commercial success within an ethical framework, both on an individual basis and collectively as an executive team. The fall out for Enron, Marconi and others aiming to put a 'spin' on corporate performance with the intention of deceiving shareholders, staff and customers are well documented examples where this expectation has not been matched. To avoid what Robert Cole (2003) in his 'Times Business' commentary has called 'Enronitis disease', applied integrity is fundamental for effective performance by those in a leadership role. Integrity has a special significance for leaders at a senior level, with the high degree of influence and accountability their role entails.

The problem is that the system in which many leaders operate can actively encourage them to abuse the trust that we place in them. The assumption we make, that a leader will behave with integrity, is often not reflected in their actual behaviour. Leaders can become prisoners of their own self-belief, of the pressures placed on them and the organisations they lead, and on the conflicting goals that they face (as happened at Enron, for example). Without their own personal integrity, these pressures can easily encourage them to believe that what they are doing is right, simply because they are doing it.

Confidence in a leader's personal attributes and his or her ability to connect with others and to build and maintain productive relationships is essential to be recognised as an effective leader and for others to follow that lead. Indeed, Boyett & Boyett's (1998) research into leadership suggested that while there are a number of characteristics associated with leadership, the one that separates leaders from non-leaders is that they have willing followers. As Robert K. Greenleaf, the man who gave the world the idea of the 'servant-leader', said:

'The only test of leadership is that somebody follows.'

Within all sizes and types of organisations, the leadership challenge at every level is to influence others towards a high performance culture. This means creating the conditions which inspire others to want to achieve corporate objectives as opposed to being driven towards them, and demands self-motivated leaders who have a high level of awareness of others. They need to be self-motivated so that they demonstrate the commitment to achieve the organisation's objectives that they want to inspire in others, and they need to be aware of others if they are to create the conditions in which people have the will to perform to the best of their ability. This is a form of 'corporate contagion' or leadership by example, where leaders' behaviour provides a role model that people don't just have the option to copy but feel motivated and empowered to replicate. Corporate contagion therefore has the maximum positive impact on the organisation culture and its performance when its leaders behave with integrity.

The vision thing

There was a problem in the provision of mental health services in South Devon in the late eighties and early nineties. They had pioneered community care and it had backfired spectacularly. A patient with mental health problems killed a social worker, and a Public Enquiry identified serious problems in the way the service was organised and run.

Dr Maggie Cork took over as the consultant psychiatrist in charge and recognised that it wasn't enough to tinker with the organisation, it needed root and branch change. The old ways of working, based on large, Victorian hospitals had to be changed in the light of the new approach to care. What's more, the change had to be made soon and they had to take everyone along with them.

The whole staff, from cleaners to consultants, as well as some patients and their carers were involved in a series of meetings at which the whole structure of care was redesigned from the bottom up. By involving everyone in the process, Dr Cork recognised that they would have an emotional investment in the new systems and procedures and new ways of working. The opportunity for everyone to talk to each other and to learn about her vision for the future of the service (based on care at home, speedy intervention, and the availability of hospital support where necessary) meant that radical change in the way that people worked was generally welcomed by those who had to make it reality.

Dr Cork describes strong leadership as being willing to *'put your head above the parapet, spell out a clear vision, a way forward as far as you can see of how the service will unfold, but to allow your embryonic views to be shaped, coloured in, influenced and even radically altered by the people you work with. Most importantly, you must be able to inspire and support people and recognise that if you are in the vanguard you will make mistakes, and be able to learn from them.'*

As Maggie Cork explains, a significant improvement in communication plus strong leadership creates a clear vision for everyone. The result? By 1999, the mental health service had been awarded Beacon Status and was being held up as an example of best practice to the healthcare system.

Earlier in **MINDCHANGE,** we suggested the abilities that leaders need as being able to:

- conceive a vision for where you want to be, based on your core values and beliefs, and communicate that vision to people in a way that convinces them to buy into this;
- see the abilities in people that they may not themselves recognise and allow them the opportunity to grow and develop these;
- be aware of your own strengths and weaknesses, and welcome the contribution of others to compensate for your limitations;
- demonstrate honesty and integrity in words and deeds;
- agree goals with people that are achievable yet stretch them to fulfil their potential, commit yourself to similar goals and work to fulfil your commitments;
- instil a sense of shared commitment with others towards the achievement of goals;
- recognise the barriers that prevent people from achieving their goals and help them to overcome these;
- be honest about your own achievements and welcome feedback from others so that you learn;
- be prepared to adapt to changing circumstances;
- win with magnanimity, lose with good grace.

None of these abilities is sufficient on its own, and none can be wholly ignored. It is the combination of all these abilities that produces the behaviour, relationships and ways of working that single out the leader from the everyday manager. These abilities are not innate, with practice and commitment all can be learnt over time, and all of them start from within potential leaders themselves in their personal desire to be effective as a leader. As we shall show, emotional intelligence is a key part of this process by helping us to understand our own feelings and those of others, and to use this understanding to shape our behaviour. It's evident from the list that many of the suggested abilities leaders need to acquire are related directly or indirectly to our own and others' emotional states.

Sometimes it seems as if leadership has only just been invented, but believe it or not, it has been the stuff of debate and discussion for at least two and a half millennia. Greek philosopher Sophocles and the Chinese philosopher Lao Tzu, both had plenty to say on the subject about it in the 5th century BC, as did Plato one hundred years later. Leadership in politics and the military has been widely studied and discussed, but leadership in an organisational setting is largely a 20th (and now 21st) century phenomenon.

Why? What is it about leadership that is so important in both commercial and non-commercial organisations these days? And why has leadership come to overshadow management in the discussions about organisational success? Is it just the latest fad in management, or is there something new, something different, today that makes leadership more important?

A thirty-year old lesson is still relevant today

Lawrence Appley was a key figure in the American Management Association and a highly influential figure in the development of management theory and practice. Back in 1974 he said that, to be effective, managers must know:

- what leadership is (the 'nature of leadership')
- how to be a leader (the 'process of leadership'), and
- the characteristics of effective leaders (the 'character of a leader')

In other words, managers need to understand leadership, they need to know how to put that understanding in to practice and, most importantly, they need to do it. Knowing about leadership and knowing how to do it, are necessary preconditions for effective leadership, but they aren't sufficient. Managers need to be leaders.

And when we look at what Appley meant when he talked about 'the characteristics of leaders' we find something that looks very similar to what we understand as emotional intelligence. He defined the characteristics of a leader as follows:

- Leaders have records of attainment (they know how they have performed, and can use this knowledge to reflect on their performance and learn from it).
- Leaders have a mission (they know where they are going, and why).
- Leaders consult (they recognise others' strengths and involve them in decision-making, using the value that comes from participation to improve both the quality of the decision-making and the ability to get decisions implemented).
- Leaders are intellectually mature (they are able to learn and to use their learning appropriately, recognising that they can't know everything being willing to find out what they need to.
- Leaders are emotionally stable (they understand their own and others emotions, and can make decisions that are informed, but not controlled, by emotions).

(Based on Lawrence Appley *'Formula for success: A core concept of management'* AMACOM: 1974)

Appley's idea of leadership as action-orientated – getting things done – is so obvious that the only surprise is how often it isn't mentioned. The idea of leadership as being goal-orientated is far more common; leadership is usually defined in terms of giving direction, having a vision, setting goals, and so on. The third dimension, the idea that leaders should think seems obvious, but there's all too often a tendency to eschew reflection and intellectual rigour in favour of action. But the idea that leaders think before they act, and think both intellectually and emotionally (that they use both their cognitive and emotional intelligence) is a key message of **MINDCHANGE**. There's an old but wise rule used by carpenters everywhere - 'measure twice, cut once'. It's the same with leadership, think things through thoroughly before taking any action.

All managers should be leaders
Another aspect of Lawrence Appley's ideas, his assumption that leadership is an integral part of being a manager, is also critical. This

is exactly what **MINDCHANGE** is all about. Managers at all levels have to be leaders, and need to recognise that being a leader is not an alternative to more conventional aspects of the management role, but an integral part of the role itself. Because, according to Charles (Chuck) Palus, of the Center for Creative Leadership, as the challenges which managers face become more complex their technical competence – their knowledge and skills – becomes less appropriate to resolve it. Technical competence is fine for continuous (incremental) improvement, isolating a specific problem and focussing resources tightly on it to find a solution. But this model doesn't suit the complexity of too many problems these days.

Complexity means that the problem has multiple causes, not just one, and is likely to require multiple changes to systems and processes, people and skills, products and services. It is unlikely that any one person can bring all the skills and knowledge needed to resolve the problem, something many managers find difficult to cope with. They see their ability to resolve problems as distinguishing them from those they manage. What they need, according to Palus, is to develop a form of leadership that he calls 'connected leadership' - a leadership which is shared with others, each of whom is able to bring a set of competencies to the problem that – jointly – will lead to its resolution. This is the arena in which emotional and cognitive intelligence interact. It's not enough to know what technical competence is needed to contribute to solving a problem, a manager also needs to know how to ensure that individuals can contribute effectively.

Complex problems require a divergent strategy, canvassing opinions and ideas from as wide a field as possible, drawing on intuition and ability to be innovative – what Cooper and Sawaf call 'emotional alchemy'. This combination of our analytical, logical and intuitive abilities demands that we are confident in using both our general intelligence and our emotional intelligence. One of the most remarkable things about humans is the gift we have to see patterns in the most confused or partial data. Yet this gift is also a curse. The patterns we look for and see are the patterns that are familiar, expected or predicted. This is where the technical strength of managers can become a weakness – they look for the things they will recognise, and see patterns that fit with their expectations. But complexity often doesn't present expected or predictable patterns, and the ability to see patterns can become a desire to impose patterns on these complex challenges.

Appley makes a similar point elsewhere in his discussion about leadership, where he argues that the *'future requires more thought than the past'*. The past was simpler, we knew how to deal with it. More significantly, we have the power of 20:20 hindsight to see things more clearly now than they may have seemed at the time. The future is only visible through a glass darkly and clouded with uncertainty, so managers and leaders have to focus on what they don't know as much as what they do know. This is what Palus means when he says we *'look for and see the patterns that are familiar, expected or predicted'*. We impose clarity on the unclear, even if it doesn't fit very well, looking to make sense where there is no sense. After all, as Plato reminded us: *'The learning and knowledge that we have, is, at the most, but little compared with that of which we are ignorant'*.

Leadership is about values

Debates about management and leadership abound, as people try to separate out the two concepts and analyse their different contributions to organisational performance. Unfortunately, all too often this becomes a sterile debate, as commentators argue about the nature and significance of the two concepts. Richard Boyatzis co-wrote *Primal Leadership* with Daniel Goleman and Annie McKee (published by Harvard Business School Press in 2002), a follow up to Goleman's ground-breaking first book on emotional intelligence exploring how emotional intelligence and leadership interact. Richard Boyatzis commented in an email interview with one of the authors in 2003 that:

'In the 50s and early 60s, we thought 'administrators' were dull, boring, and ineffective – we wanted managers. In the late 60s and 70s, we thought managers were dull, boring, and ineffective – we wanted leaders. In the 80s and early 90s, we thought leaders were dull, boring, and ineffective – we wanted transformational leaders.... But seriously, people are escalating their titles but the need is the

roughly the same. We want people who inspire us.'

It's not the name – administrators, managers or leaders – but the need for inspirational figures that matters. Why? Because, as he also commented: *'...as the environment has gotten more uncertain and less clear as to how to 'win'... we have lost confidence in all of our social institutions ... we don't know who or what to believe in. So we turned to our work organisations and expected, or hoped, that the leaders would provide more meaning for us than before.'*

If, as Richard Boyatzis suggests, we aren't getting the leadership we expect from the social or political organisations, then perhaps we expect more from the organisations we work for and deal with? Of course, not everyone is happy with this idea of management and leadership as somehow being interlinked. There are many who think the two are quite distinct concepts; Richard Boyatzis referred to this in his comment about 'transformational leadership'.

The idea of transformational leadership originated with James MacGregor Burns, an American historian and political scientist, who was interested in leadership in its broader context of leading societies and nations, and who distinguished between 'transactional' and 'transformational' leaders. For him, true leadership was about being driven by morality, by ethical values and goals, because *'naked power-wielding can be neither transformational nor transactional; only leadership can be'.*

Transactional leaders focus on the means (the transactions) to achieve their goals, ensuring that these are fair and reflect the leaders' moral values. Transformational leaders are focused on the ends, the moral goals that are to be attained, such as truth, justice or freedom. As Burns' ideas have been adapted in management, the two styles of leadership have often been reduced to:

'Doing things right' - Transactional leadership

This is about ensuring that actions are ethically correct or, more prosaically, that resources are employed efficiently and effectively and in accord with the appropriate rules and procedures. It assumes that the values have been set by others and that the procedures are in place. Transactional leadership simply makes sure that things are done the way they are supposed to be done, without questioning the rightness of those values or procedures.

'Doing the right thing' – Transformational leadership

This is about setting and achieving goals, defining the values that guide the organisation and then implementing those values. It is also about coping with change in an increasingly uncertain environment, by using the values and goals of the organisation to provide some of certainty, like a light shining in the darkness to guide people where they need to go.

This – perhaps over-simple – distinction was originally used by Warren Bennis to distinguish between leadership ('doing the right thing') and management ('doing things right'). Having paraphrased leadership and management down to these two rather trite statements, the further conclusion is also drawn, that 'leadership' (transformation) is all about change whilst 'management' is simply about making sure that things work properly (transactions). Given the speed and frequency of change these days, (transformational) leadership has become seen as the necessary behaviour, and management (transactional leadership) is seen as being old-fashioned, resistant to change, and encouraging the retention of the status quo. In other words, leadership good, management bad!

This emphasis on leadership as being a more dynamic, change-orientated role and management as being a bit fuddy-duddy, all about systems and procedures, may simplify commentators' attitudes and opinions. A prejudice against management and towards leadership may not be relevant in the long term, if all we are doing is re-labelling the same basic competences. After all, what we call it doesn't matter, as long as the function is needed and performed well.

> *'When I use a word,'* Humpty Dumpty said, in rather a scornful tone, *'it means just what I choose it to mean - neither more nor less.'*
>
> *'The question is,'* said Alice, *'whether you can make words mean so many different things.'*
>
> (*'Through the Looking Glass'*, Lewis Carroll)

However, if there is a meaningful distinction to be made between leadership and management, and if both functions are a necessary (if not essential) part of successful organisational performance, then the distinction between the two is significant and worth exploring. We believe it is. In our view, leadership is an intrinsic part of effective management, and that without the ability to demonstrate effective and appropriate leadership skills, managers won't achieve what they – and the people they manage – are capable of. Rather than Humpty Dumpty, we prefer the words of Colin Powell, former US Secretary of State, in his autobiography *'A Soldier's Way'* (2001), *'The way I like to put it, leadership is the art of accomplishing more than the science of management says is possible'*.

What sort of leader?

How people lead other people – their leadership style – has been the centre of debate for a very long time. The textbooks are full of choices of leadership styles. One of the original models is Rensis Likert's 1967 (in his ground-breaking book *'The Human Organization: Its Management and Value'*) set of four leadership styles:

- **Exploitative – authoritative**, where decisions made high up and are imposed on subordinates who learn do what they're told, or else.
- **Benevolent – authoritative**, which has a similar approach but leaders care about you when they tell you what to do!
- **Consultative leadership**, which is a bit more open and involving, but ultimate responsibility still rests at the top.
- **Participative – group**, where goals are jointly agreed in an open and trusting environment.

Three years earlier, Robert Blake and Jane Moulton came up with a similar set in their book *The Managerial Grid*. They thought that the two main dimensions that characterised leadership styles were people/relationships and task. Some people focused on the one, some on the other. The best leaders, like Likert's Participative – group style, are team leaders who combine both a strong people and a strong task emphasis (see illustration).

Blake and Moulton's Managerial Grid

Paul Hersey and Kenneth Blanchard developed the Management Grid to propose their 'Situational Leadership' model. Situational leadership (also described as contingency theory) suggests that leaders should be able to adopt an appropriate leadership style to suit the situation they find themselves in. They use the same two key attributes, *task* focus and *people/relationship* focus, and identify four styles which might just remind you of Likert's:

- **Directive** (telling) leaders expect subordinates to do as they are told
- **Supportive** (selling) leaders are more friendly and show concern for subordinates
- **Participative** leaders consult subordinates and listen to their ideas.
- **Delegative** leaders encourage subordinates to agree goals, make decisions and control their own work

More recently, Daniel Goleman, Richard Boyatzis and Annie McKee, in *'The New Leaders'* (Little, Brown: 2003), describe six different leadership styles.

Style	Characteristics
1. **Visionary**	Move people towards shared dreams, create a sense of direction, encourage change
2. **Coaching**	Helps improve performance and align theirs and the organisation's goals
3. **Affiliative**	Builds relationships and teams, heals tensions and helps deal with problem situations
4. **Democratic**	Helps create buy-in or consensus by involving people and valuing their input
5. **Pacesetting**	Sets challenges that high performers can achieve but can leave stragglers in the wake
6. **Commanding**	Good in a crisis, calms things down and gives direction when problems arise

Goleman, Boyatzis and McKee also argue that good leaders can adopt the style that suits the moment (i.e., situational leadership). But, they argue, the key to selecting the most appropriate style is having well developed emotional intelligence.

But there's more to it than that, because they believe that not all the leadership styles are quite as safe to use as others. The problem is 'resonance', or rather the lack of it. Resonance is about being attuned to people's feelings or emotions, something that emotionally intelligent people are able to do. The first four styles (Visionary,

Coaching, Affiliative and Democratic) encourage resonance, and enable the leaders to be in tune with the people they lead. Visionaries encourage the development of shared dreams, coaches align individuals with the organisation, affiliative leaders create harmony between people and democrats gain commitment.

That's the good news. Resonant styles are a sort of 'easy listening' style of leadership, creating harmony and encouraging leaders and their teams to be in tune with each other. However, the other two styles (Pacesetting and Commanding) are more like the punk rock of leadership, creating discordance and dissonance. Pacesetting is risky because only the brave and the best survive the challenges that pacesetters can conjure up, and commanding leaders are really only appropriate in a crisis. Pacesetters tend to be people who are themselves high achievers, who set demanding goals for themselves and get a buzz out of achieving those goals. David McClelland described a similar style some 50 years ago as Achievement-motivated managers, who were really only interested in the tasks and how well they were performing on it. The style is also a bit like Blake and Moulton's Authoritarian leaders, but without some of the negative characteristics they ascribed to them.

The reason that Pacesetters create dissonance is that they are impatient with people who can't keep up and tend to take over the tasks for themselves. Commanding leaders are less likely to take over but are more likely to kick people out. The attraction of commanding leadership is that it is easier to tell than it is to sell, and much easier than consulting and letting people participate. The result is that the commanding style all too easily descends into authoritarianism, an approach that's not encouraged by Likert, Blake & Moulton nor Hersey & Blanchard.

But it's questionable if the commanding (or authoritarian) style is right even in a crisis. Jeff odgers, a Director of Cirrus Highland Ltd and a specialist in crisis management, challenges the assumption that when a crisis occurs managers should *'forget everything they have learned on management courses, disregard hard-earned management experience and lead. By which people usually mean, be directive, decisive, confidant, all-knowing and, above all, right!'*

He argues that *'it is easy to be blinded by the differences between routine operations and crisis and to see people as needing to change in order to cope – to use new skills rather than adapting those already well practised. It could be argued instead that a crisis situation provides a perfect opportunity to combine leadership and management skills; that the application of some mainstream management skills can have a positive effect in the resolution of a crisis situation.'* By mainstream management skills he means planning what you are going to do, trusting your team, allowing them to make decisions when they are better placed to make them, and consulting them for information, experience and advice.

If you are beginning to feel confused, perhaps you should be. If all these different leadership styles are saying more or less the same thing and arguing that there's really just a single set of skills that should be deployed as appropriate, then effective leadership can be summed up as having the right skills and being able to judge when to use them; which brings us to Professor Gerry Randell, Emeritus Professor of the University of Bradford Management Centre. His argument is that a lot of what is talked about leadership is a way of avoiding the harsh truth, that leadership is applied management.

Randall's view is that management is about knowing what is the right thing to do, leadership is about being able to apply that knowledge and, given that this generally involves getting people to do something, relies heavily on people skills. He doesn't mince his words, either:

'Unfortunately these views have not been faced up to enough, even ignored, so that managers have been led to believe by academics, consultants and even government quangos that leadership is attitude, belief, confidence, vision and all the other slippery concepts, which has made it easy for people to get enthusiastic about it as these are apparently easy to acquire. So the current popularity (of leadership, as opposed to management) is probably due to the non-threatening promulgations that are made in all the leadership books piled up at airports! If managers only realised that to become an EFFECTIVE leader of people, not just a captain of industry, they would have to first expose themselves to their own inadequacies and then take on time-consuming practice to overcome them.'

We have developed a mechanism through which you can apply this principle. By using the **MINDCHANGE EQ4U** process you can focus on those areas in which you need to develop and improve your performance. We don't pretend that it makes you a leader overnight, but that what it does is to set you on the road to leadership by helping you to understand your own emotional state and that of others so that you can appreciate how your leadership practice affects you and others.

Management is leadership, leadership is management

It's too easy to see the management role as mundane and inferior to the leader's role. Drawing up plans, budgets and work schedules; organising operational systems and workflows, and drawing up timetables and rosters; setting tasks and imposing discipline; making sure that different elements of the organisation or the team work together; monitoring individual or group performance and seeking to improve it. Somehow it doesn't have the same cachet as John Kotter's description of leadership as:

- Establishing direction – developing a vision of the future, and the strategies to create it;
- Aligning people – communicating direction in words and deeds to everyone whose cooperation is needed to create the vision;
- Motivating and inspiring – energising people to overcome major political, bureaucratic, and resource barriers to change by satisfying basic, but often unfulfilled, human needs

(John P. Kotter *'Leading Change'* McGraw-Hill: 1996)

...or Kouzes and Posner's 'five leadership practices':

- Challenge the Process
- Inspire a Shared Vision
- Enable Others to Act
- Model the Way
- Encourage the Heart

98

(James M. Kouzes and Barry Z. Posner *'The Leadership Challenge'* Jossey Bass Wiley: 2003)

These are inspirational ideas, which is no doubt what makes them attractive (if hard to practice). That's the thing about leaders – leaders inspire. Leaders provide meaning. Leadership is that quality that makes people want to head in a particular direction, want to achieve goals. It is about confidence, belief and a sense of being able to make things happen. Above all, leadership is what enables ordinary people to do extraordinary things.

It's not enough for leaders to inspire confidence and belief in them, as leaders. They need to inspire people to have confidence and belief in themselves, because leaders don't do things by themselves, leaders enable other people to do things.

By contrast, managers may feel that they rarely have the opportunity to inspire. For them, there may seem to be nothing inspirational about drawing up a holiday rota, a business plan or a job description. On the other hand, how can you inspire your team if you ruin their holiday plans? How do you set a direction if you don't have the resources in place to make the journey possible? And it's difficult to inspire confidence if you're off to the Employment Tribunal to face a complaint of discrimination in your recruitment process, when you can't even say what the job involves. It can also be argued that developing a business plan requires not only an analytical mindset, but also a need to stimulate and inspire others to want to follow the route and achieve the stated business objectives.

So, let's get away from looking at management and leadership as alternative ways of 'getting things done', one good one bad, or management as the lower level standard and leadership as a higher level. Instead, let's think of leadership and management as two complementary elements of the same overall function. Like the two faces on a coin, the heads and the tails, the two components are different but inseparable. Effective leadership depends on effective management, and vice-versa, a combination of disciplined organisation of the tasks and inspiration of the people performing them.

Management and leadership levels

However, the way that these two components – management and leadership – are combined varies according to the nature or level of the role. The balance of leadership to management, the extent to which the functional role demands 'planning, organising, commanding, coordinating and controlling' (Fayol's classical management roles) on the one hand, and establishing direction, aligning people, motivating and inspiring them (leadership à la Kotter on the other), will vary in scale and balance.

The range of management levels runs from the directors (or elected members of councils), senior managers and executives at the top to the people leading the teams of people who actually produce or deliver goods and services. (We know that in organisations committed to TQM, IiP, etc, the pyramid is inverted, but we have shown it this way up in the diagram on page 107 to reflect the hierarchy of organisational power, no matter how it is wielded.)

While it could be argued that there's a role distinction between directors and senior managers (as emphasised in the Institute of Directors' publication *'The Effective Director'*, edited by Chris Pierce), we have integrated these into a senior management classification because of the overlap in abilities their roles demand. How we designate these levels also varies according to the size, structure and complexity of the organisation, but for simplicity we are going to identify three distinct levels. These are based upon a belief that while the balance of management and leadership behaviours expected from role holders is common within each level, there are significant variations between the three levels.

1. Senior managers

These are the CEOs, Directors and others operating at a similar, predominately strategic, level in organisations who have specific responsibility for setting its direction and who have the greatest span of control and breadth of responsibility. They perform the broadest management function and the broadest leadership function, with a significant emphasis on the latter. This reflects their primary orientation towards setting direction and ensuring that the organisation is structured and resourced so that it is aligned with the direction, and that the mechanisms are in place to motivate people. Above all, they must establish and demonstrate the values and attributes that inspire people to make their goals happen.

Senior managers will be responsible for attracting and negotiating for new investment or other external funding streams and accountable for the return on capital investment and with meeting broad and longer term goals. They are likely to have full budgetary accountability for their area of responsibility and can authorise large items of expenditure. Individuals may be responsible for entire operating divisions or whole organisations. They will all have wide spans of control, measured in hundreds or even thousands in some cases, and will have extensive influence over all employees. Their role demands that they can manage the resources and people they control, and that they can lead people towards achieving agreed goals.

They will be concerned primarily with future requirements and changes in systems, operations and performance. Their performance will be measured against objectives based on aggregates of activity, such as total revenue or output and the achievement of the goals that they have agreed. The ability to look to the future and set ambitious but achievable goals, and to accept accountability for their achievement, are critical leadership abilities.

Senior managers will have operational managers reporting to them and will be accountable for the performance of those managers and their people. They may also be involved in the recruitment, promotion and discipline of operational managers and senior technical or professional staff, and with their performance management. In fact, effective leadership of an organisation involves ensuring that the people you directly manage are able to develop and learn under your tutelage.

In large organisations, there may well be several more tiers of management between senior managers and front line people, and they need to be alert not just to the effect their decisions and their behaviour has on those they work most immediately with, but also those at a distance. The ability to empathise with people you haven't met, to appreciate how your actions will play out when they impact on others you don't know, is demanding and requires a high level emotional intelligence that is often found challenging.

Senior managers may negotiate directly with major customers and suppliers, on the broad terms and conditions of contracts, and on details and prices in some instances (especially with capital good markets). They may also be responsible for negotiating with other organisations on the development of jointly owned ventures and mergers or transfers of undertakings. Their ability to inspire confidence and trust, intrinsic qualities of effective leaders, will be crucial in this aspect of their role.

The senior managers may regard themselves as (and may actually operate as) a team. Indeed, in a number of circumstances, such as a project team consisting of senior managers, the term 'Team Leader' may even be recognised as a designation for the manager leading the project. We won't however refer to this group as team leaders, because we want to save that label for another specific role. However, the ability of senior managers to work as a team is likely to reflect their leadership capability because, as we have said, leaders should be 'aware of their own strengths and weaknesses and welcome the contribution of others to compensate for their limitations'.

2. Operational managers

Operational managers (which includes such categories often defined as middle and first line managers) represent the core of any management structure, the people who convert strategy into action, who make the organisation work (or not, as the case may be). It includes a wide swathe of managers who have a responsibility for translating the goals set by senior managers into practice, by establishing, operating, controlling and monitoring procedures – a strong task-focus. They are also required to communicate the vision and ensure that the motivation and inspiration are there. If senior managers provide strong leadership, operational managers help to make sure that things happen in response.

The emphasis on action and the focus of their time tends to be highly functional – designing and operating systems. This can often lead to these managers ignoring the leadership dimension of their role because it seems to be redundant. Leadership is too abstract and forward-looking; they are having to deal with the day to day, the here and now. What's more, if senior managers provide weak leadership, operational managers are unable to compensate; they can at best give some structure within which people can work, but it is likely to be inward looking and compensatory (replacing the vigour that good leadership from the top provides) rather than outward looking and supportive (reinforcing strong leadership from the top).

While the balance of their time may be towards management, this does not mean that leadership is non-existent, nor does it mean it is not important. Joseph Juran, the giant, along with W Edwards Deming, of the post-war quality revolution, has a lovely description of the position that operational managers occupy. Senior managers, says Juran, speak the language of money because it is only through money that the whole organisation and its operations can be described and measured. Resources, facilities, equipment, output, all can be expressed in one common measure, and that makes it possible for senior managers to make sense of the organisation as a whole.

Front line personnel, the people who actually produce the goods and services, speak the language of 'things'. For them the organisation is experienced as cars on the production line, insurance claims or planning applications processed, customers served, patients treated. This is the reality of the organisation for them. Operational managers therefore have to be bi-lingual. They must communicate with senior managers in the language they understand, and also with the people they manage in their language.

But operational managers are not just translators; they must also be communicators, originating their own messages and analysing and revising the messages they pass on. One of the features of the emotionally intelligent leader is to recognise how people will react to a message and to ensure that it is accepted and understood in a positive and constructive way. After all, operational managers are accountable for the performance of all those over whom they have control, directly or indirectly, and they have a responsibility for ensuring that people understand what is expected of them and where they are headed.

Characteristic of the role is the responsibility for allocating resources and for recruiting, promoting and disciplining people, and for engaging in direct negotiation with internal and external customers and suppliers, underpinning their accountability for the quality of the goods or services supplied. They are also likely to engage in leadership of projects to bring about changes in products, services, resources or systems.

All this demands knowledge – technical knowledge about markets, processes, people and equipment. It also means knowledge about the history of the organisation and the industry they operate in, as this shapes the present and the likely future, about which they are also expected to have some awareness.

During the early nineties, large organisations in the UK, the USA and elsewhere entered into a frenzy of down-sizing and de-layering, encouraged by an often poorly-understood attempt at business process re-engineering. De-layering, a simple label for a complex and highly risky organisational strategy, involved stripping out layers of management on the assumption that they were unproductive, reducing value.

One immediate consequence was the loss of knowledge; knowledge about suppliers, about processes, about customers and about people. Knowledge is the resource that makes an organisation function; without knowledge, it is simply a collection of resources. There is no co-ordination, planning is uninformed about what will work and what won't. The role of operational managers is to enable those resources to work well, to produce the quality of goods and services that customers require, to do so efficiently and at minimal cost, on time, every time. No mean feat. Their ability to perform this role is often dependent on a detailed understanding of the people they manage, and how they will react to particular circumstances and events, based on their technical knowledge and skills, and also their emotional intelligence, their insight and intuition honed by years of working in the shared environment and dealing with people on a day to day basis.

Operational managers may also frequently find themselves as leaders of project teams of one sort or another, depending on their level of responsibility and technical specialism. In this role they may find that they have to demonstrate the leadership skills of the team leader (below), as they will perhaps be working with people who are of the same level of responsibility as themselves. Although their management skills may be significant in ensuring that the project is operationally sound and delivered successfully, their principal role in this context will be that of leadership.

3. Team leaders

Team leader is used to describe those who lead and supervise the front line people responsible for producing the goods or delivering the services that the organisation exists to produce or deliver. In some ways team leaders are like senior managers in having a predominately leadership role. However their management responsibility is minimal since their planning is very short term, they have very few resources to organise, and while they do have to co-ordinate, their command and control function is generally limited. In the main, the team leader's role is to set clear goals (direction), make sure their team members are all on board (aligned), and then motivate and inspire them to get things done (perform).

Team leaders operate at the sharp end of the organisation, and are first and foremost part of the team that they also lead. Being leaders of teams adds to their primary role, which is to do whatever it is the rest of the team are also doing. The team leader's focus is on the very short term, on the day-to-day performance of the team and its members. They have responsibility for allocating tasks between team members, for ensuring that individuals are supported in their performance of their job role and that what is being produced conforms to the requirements of the organisation and its customers. Their role also includes a significant communication role, between the team and its managers.

Most team leaders have very little position power, the power to command, in a traditional, authoritarian sense. They cannot threaten punishment because they usually don't have the authority to punish someone who fails to carry out their tasks as directed. Instead they must rely heavily on their personal power to affect how people perform. If they need to take more commanding action they must report someone to a manager, but in doing so they will often lose any personal power they have, unless the 'crime' is recognised as serious enough to warrant such draconian action. Because team leaders rely on their personal power for much of their authority, it is their role to get things done by leading, not by controlling.

EQ4U and management levels

While distinctions have been made between the three levels in the way described, we are not saying that the people at the top and bottom are leaders and those in the middle are managers. Nor are we saying that the role of the team leader and the CEO is essentially the same. (It's too easy for complex ideas about management and leadership to be reduced to simplistic dichotomies, either/or statements that ignore the subtleties of the situation.) Finally, we must emphasise that these distinctions are nothing like as clear-cut in practice as they are made to appear. The reality is one of shades of distinction between the different roles and levels.

However, what we are saying is that the balance between those parts of the role that are generally classed as management and those that are generally classed as leadership varies through these different levels. The predominantly management tasks include such responsibilities as obtaining resources, organising work, designing systems and procedures, monitoring performance, maintaining and improving resources, systems and procedures, etc. The leadership tasks include developing a vision and setting direction, building commitment and harnessing abilities to achieve the vision, motivating people, building relationships, etc. The following diagram shows this variability.

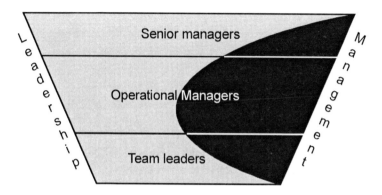

The management/leadership balance

The diagram shows how the magnitude of the role increases from team leader to CEO in terms of the scale of responsibility, the complexity of decision-making and the scope of the role. Team leaders have limited responsibility for a small number of people undertaking largely unchanging tasks. CEOs have full responsibility for all aspects of the organisation's strategy and operations and constantly deal with novel or unpredictable situations.

At the same time, the balance between those aspects of the role that can be described as management and those that can be described as leadership vary in the way we have identified. People in leadership and management roles at all levels in organisations need to possess both leadership and management competences. What's more, they need to use these skills in ways that are appropriate to the situation facing them. Some call for a predominantly management role, others for predominantly leadership role. Many (if not most) demand a mix of both.

However, it is likely that the tasks that a senior manager faces will tend to demand a predominantly leadership role, whereas the department manager will need to focus far more on the management role in ensuring that the systems and procedures needed to make the organisation function effectively are in place and are operated properly. Having said that, the department manager must also lead the department, just as the CEO must secure the finances and structure the organisation to achieve the goals set. However, it is primarily in the leadership role that emotional intelligence has the most significant role to play, and it is worth exploring how this plays out at each of these different levels.

EQ4U is not a description of emotional intelligence, but a process – one that can guide you in addressing the wide range of issues that you will face as a manager and leader. You can use the descriptions of the different management levels to help you make sense of your role and to recognise the mix of management and leadership qualities, skills and abilities that you need to perform effectively. However, to understand fully how emotional intelligence relates to your specific role, we have used **EQ4U** to assess each of these different levels.

This analysis is in **Reflections Explored Part 4: Developing EQ4U Leadership**. You can use this to reflect on your role and your own performance in it, especially on your level of emotional competence (applied emotional intelligence). The remainder of Part 4 will help you to identify ways of developing and improving your performance, but before that, in **Reflections Explored Part 3: Exploring Leadership Practice**, we offer you the chance to see how the emotional competence of some managers and leaders has enabled organisations to succeed in often very challenging circumstances. You will also recognise in the case studies outlined, how the lack of emotional competence has been detrimental to others.

Reflections Explored
Part 3:
Leadership Practice

Introduction

'Traditional management teaches that leaders ought to be cool, aloof and analytical; they ought to separate emotion from work. Yet when real life leaders discuss what they're the proudest of in their careers, they describe feelings of inspiration, passion, elation, intensity, challenge, caring and kindness – and yes, even love.'
James Kouzes and Barry Posner, *'The Leadership Challenge'*

We have chosen the following case studies to illustrate the significant influence that leadership behaviour can have (both positively and negatively) on the process and outcomes involved. Our collection includes a range of scenarios, with varying degrees of applied emotional intelligence demonstrated by the leaders involved.

Personal experience of working with clients, direct accounts from others and our own research are incorporated in reporting the process and outcomes outlined within these. We have not named some of the people or, in one case, the organisation concerned, for reasons of confidentiality. All five case studies reflect real people, organisations and events; we must stress, however, that the conclusions and key learning points we have drawn from each of the case studies are ours alone and their incorporation here does not necessarily imply endorsement or even agreement by the individuals and organisations concerned.

Each one of the case studies reviews the degree of application of emotionally intelligent leadership behaviour and its impact on the people, the situation and the organisation concerned. Wider implications of leadership behaviour are also reflected on and conclusions drawn on key learning points. *'Corporate contagion'* - the effect of leaders' behaviour on others is a key theme throughout.

To provide a straightforward analysis of each situation, leadership behaviour within the case studies is summed up by mapping against the **EQ4U PROCESS MODEL** introduced in Part 1 of, 'Reflections Explored'. While the model suggests individual and personalised analysis and application, it can also be applied on a collective basis within a shared leadership context. To work effectively however within a shared leadership situation, a constructive, open and honest teamwork approach is essential.

To remind you, the **EQ4U PROCESS MODEL** has three elements:

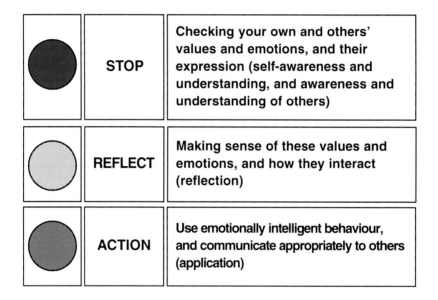

The three elements incorporate four stages.

Stage 1 – Self-awareness and understanding

- Awareness and acknowledgement of own body language 'signals' and associated emotions
- Understanding own emotions ~ listening to and reflecting on intuitive feelings *(gut reactions)*

Stage 2 – Awareness and understanding of others

- Being interested in and aware of others' body language and behaviours
- Interpreting and anticipating others' emotions within the overall context of the situation

Stage 3 – Reflection

Reflection on:

- an ethical framework of principles and values.
- the overall situational context including own and others' circumstances.
- own emotions and others' anticipated emotions.
- communication that will:
  - ⇨ demonstrate recognition and understanding of the context;
  - ⇨ be clearly and appropriately communicated;
  - ⇨ be genuine, open and honest; and
  - ⇨ show an appropriate degree of warmth.

Stage 4 – EQ Application

Responding with behaviour that reflects:

- recognition of own and others' emotions
- a match with ethical principles and values
- a relevant communication protocol.

While the model aims to provide a simple framework against which to assess both own and others' behaviour; in reality, situational complexities inevitably mean that objective assessment is problematic, particularly when we are involved in assessing our own behaviour! We believe however, that using the model to either plan an approach or make an assessment after the event will be of value in a range of both work and personal situational contexts, and that this applies both to the individual leader and to the leadership team.

Because EQ is about people's behaviour and how they deal with own and others' emotions (rather than technical or managerial processes and systems), our emphasis is on personal approaches and leadership style. We also reflect on the difference in context between operational issues, internal politics and culture, and how people's behaviour is affected by these. Each case study incorporates a comparison of perceived leadership behaviour of those involved against elements of the EQ model and the impact on others as a result of this, and concludes with key learning points.

Leadership and management decision-making and behaviour within large corporate multi-nationals invariably has wide implications in terms of overall numbers of people affected. Strategic leadership impact in a large corporation may however be lessened because of the larger numbers and levels in leadership roles. Potential for increased impact of leadership influence lies therefore within small/medium enterprises or divisions of larger companies where leadership roles are more likely to include both strategy and operations.

The case studies have been chosen to reflect a range and depth of learning points relevant to leaders at all levels and within all types of organisations, and are intended to be of interest to both strategic and operational leadership practice. Practical examples of application are included, i.e. how to apply emotional intelligence and how to challenge behaviour assertively where it does not match EQ in practice. Researching and writing up the case studies has in any case been a valuable learning experience and a significant reminder of what can be achieved through emotionally competent leadership.

Case Study 1:
The Latin American Dilemma

'Dedicated to advancing the inner side of leadership and successful enterprise in which how we do business together is as important as what we produce, and how we serve others is as vital as how much we profit.'
Robert Cooper and Ayman Sawaf, *'Executive EQ'*

Introduction

How do you cope when you are on the point of securing a major order and, without warning, something happens that threatens to scupper the whole deal. Do you profess ignorance, in the hope that your customer hasn't heard about it, or do you face up to the problem and deal with it? To a large extent, the answer will depend on the quality of the relationship with the customer. It's now too late to start trying to build trust, you have to have it in place and be able to draw on it if you want to work out a solution together.

This was the dilemma facing a team from British Aerospace (now BAe Systems), as they heard the news that threatened to scupper a multi-million pound order and make three years work a waste of time.

The story

It was early December, in 1987, and a team from British Aerospace (BAe) in Santiago had been engaged in a sales campaign targeted at the Chilean airline LADECO for the last 18 months (although some of the initial contacts and discussions stretched back over the previous three years). The campaign had already cost around $5m and its objective was to persuade the board and management of the airline to buy a number of BAe 146-200 Series aeroplanes for use on their developing regional route network throughout Latin America. Such a sale, worth around £265 million at today's values, would represent a major breakthrough for the type in this region, and was likely to lead to further sales opportunities with other airlines in the region. A successful sales campaign would have a significant impact on the aircraft's future, and on the jobs of the workforce at Woodford and Hatfield. It was also critical for the careers of the staff involved in the sales campaign who were conscious that they were being carefully watched by BAe's senior managers.

The campaign was being fought against a background of fierce competition from Boeing with the B737-500 Series, McDonnell-Douglas with the MD-87 and Fokker with the F-28, although the latter had now effectively dropped out of the competition. The intensity of the campaign had been compounded by both the internal political situation within LADECO (between the management and shareholders), the wider political situation in Chile, and the Byzantine decision-making processes within the region in general.

As a further background consideration it needs to be remembered that communications in this part of the world, in 1987, were still relatively primitive. The internet, e-mails, global mobile phones, laptop computers, satellite television channels, CNN etc. were all still future developments. Landline calls or telex via hotel operators were the norm.

This was not a simple sales situation. There were complex business, political and personal interrelationships between the various parties involved in the campaign, including various government ministers and senior civil servants, Chilean bankers, lawyers, and the local aviation regulatory authorities. The result was that although there were players within the airline in favour of the 146, there were also a number of key players thought to be in favour of the rival Boeing or McDonnell-Douglas planes.

All decisions so far had been arrived at tortuously and had not necessarily enjoyed the outright endorsement of all the parties

115

involved. The BAe project team had been camped out at the Sheraton San Cristobel Hotel for the last 5 weeks. Collectively very tired, having been working pretty continuously under enormous pressure over this period, they were now looking forward to being home for Christmas. They had finally achieved a position where their proposal had been approved by the management, by the board and by the shareholders of the airline. It had also been sanctioned by the Chilean Government, (which was also a shareholder) and the commercial, legal and financial team had been working continuously, finalising contract details with their opposite numbers in the airline. Despite this, both the Boeing and McDonnell-Douglas teams remained 'camped out' at nearby hotels and were in a continuing dialogue with various members of the LADECO management. They would not give up the fight until a contract was publicly announced and they were absolutely sure the battle was lost.

However, the Executive Board of LADECO had agreed that they would sign the contract at a ceremony in their Board Room at 18:00 hrs on the 7th December, and this would be followed by a small champagne reception. After the reception, most of the BAe team planned to catch the last evening flight to Buenos Aires, to connect with a flight to Miami and from there back to the UK. A number of the LADECO team had also indicated their intention to be leaving Santiago shortly on other business or personal commitments.

With 35 minutes to go before this signing ceremony, the BAe Business Director leading the sales team received a call from the BAe Regional Operations Director in Washington DC, in the USA. He has called with 'some bad news'. He had just received a call from a contact within the Federal Aviation Authority advising him of an initial report that *'a BAe 146 operated by Pacific Southwest Airlines (PSA) has crashed near Paso Robles in California. There are unlikely to be any survivors'*. He had very little additional further information other than the accident happened some 50 minutes into the flight, in good weather conditions, when it would have been at cruise altitude.

Pilot error seemed unlikely, although not impossible, and a midair collision was also a possibility but again unlikely as the flight was under 'positive radar coverage' from Oakland Centre and they had reported no other aircraft in the vicinity. The flight was en route directly to Los Angeles, following the US coastline, and well clear of any mountains. The crash raised the spectre of a catastrophic airframe, engine or systems failure, like the De Havilland Comet tragedies of the 1950s, although this would have been the first crash of the type since the 146 entered airline service about 18 months earlier.

The Business Director had barely 20 minutes to get the BAe team together and decide what to do. Taxis for the trip to LADECO HQ were booked for 17.45 from the hotel and it would take approximately 10 minutes to get there – to be late would be unacceptable. Clearly his immediate concern was to protect the deal and ensure the contract was signed according to the agreed timetable. He pulled the team together and told them quickly and simply what he knew and asked for their input. Views and advice ranged across a wide continuum. Some thought the team should not disclose any knowledge of this accident, having no idea whatsoever of the cause, in the hope LADECO haven't heard about it yet! Others suggested asking for a delay in the contract signing ceremony, and still others thought they should tell LADECO all they knew and ask them what they wanted to do.

Having listened to this, and with time rapidly running out, the Business Director asked the Commercial Director and Chief Training Captain to join him in the taxi to the airline. He had two questions for them:

1. How could they maintain the integrity of this contract?
2. Was a major failure a real possibility?

They agreed the latter was highly unlikely; the Chief Training Captain said: *'This is a very strong aeroplane in all respects. I am fully confident we will rapidly establish that this is not the cause'*. It was agreed that the Commercial Director would write a short letter to the LADECO President simply saying that if the subsequent official report into the PSA accident found it was attributable to a major design fault in the 146, then without penalty to LADECO, the contract would become null and void at their request.

117

He then handwrote this in the back of the taxi, in both English and Spanish. When the team arrived at the airline offices, the Business Director asked for a few minutes privately with the company's President. He told him exactly what he was aware of and that no more than that was known. He also advised the company President that he had no reason to believe the aeroplane was at fault, but to safeguard his position as a customer, BAe were offering the side letter agreed in the taxi.

The LADECO President then called in his Commercial Director and they briefly discussed the letter and, with a few minor changes, agreed to sign it. The contract signing ceremony then went ahead as planned and the team returned home very tired but pleased, having slept virtually all the way back from Santiago to London.

Several weeks later, in London, LADECO's President confided that he had heard of the accident report some time shortly before the BAe team arrived, via a family member based in Miami. It had appeared as a newsflash on NBC. He had thought the BAe team might not have heard the news in any case, and decided at the time to mention it only to his Commercial Director. LADECO's President also confided that the way the BAe Business Director and his team had handled this had convinced him and several of his other directors (who had been against the 146 deal) that they had made the right decision.

The subsequent accident investigation became a FBI investigation within 48 hours, with a clear cause. A disgruntled former PSA employee had killed his former supervisor, who was on board the aircraft, and then killed both pilots, causing the crash in which all 38 passengers and five crew members were killed.

The EQ4U Process Model

What does this tell us about emotional intelligence? First, that the relationships built between individuals over a long period of time had led them to trust each other, on both sides. The BAe team believed that if they were honest and straightforward they would be believed and that the LADECO executives would respond in the same spirit, as was the case. The LADECO executives had learnt to trust and respect them because of their behaviour over the previous 18 months or more, and responded in the way they did because of this.

Self-awareness and understanding

- Awareness and acknowledgement of own body language 'signals' and associated emotions
- Understanding own emotions ~ listening to and reflecting on intuitive feelings *(gut reactions)*

This reflected the team's self-awareness and their willingness to work with their gut feelings about what was the right thing to do. There are many managerial models of decision-making based on assessment of the scenario, with projections of the probable outcomes and likely success of alternative decisions. These are all valid in their way but positively unhelpful in the situation facing the BAe team. They had far too little information or time to consider the alternatives or assess the probabilities associated with them. All they could do was to go with what felt right.

Awareness and understanding of others

- Being interested in and aware of others' body language and behaviours
- Interpreting and anticipating others' emotions within the overall context of the situation

It also reflected their awareness of others. They had got to know their opposite numbers in the airline and they understood the conflicting pressures there and the implications of adding further reasons for putting off or even changing the decision. Nevertheless, they believed that the LADECO President would make a fair decision and that by not trying to deceive him they would strengthen their position, not weaken it.

Reflection

Reflection on:

- an ethical framework of principles and values.
- the overall situational context including own and others' circumstances.
- own emotions and others' anticipated emotions.
- communication that will:
  - ⇨ demonstrate recognition and understanding of the context;
  - ⇨ be clearly and appropriately communicated;
  - ⇨ be genuine, open and honest; and
  - ⇨ show an appropriate degree of warmth

In arriving at the decision to do what they did, the Business Director was demonstrating reflection. His behaviour was clearly ethical, in that he realised that being honest was the right and proper thing to do. He considered the overall situation, particularly the circumstances for the Chilean team and the need to ensure that none of them was put at a disadvantage by either revealing the accident or by trying to cover it up. Given the complex emotional states at the time of the signing, he needed to present the LADECO team with a proposal that would be calming rather than reignite the differences of opinion that still lay beneath the surface. Finally, he used his good personal relationship with the LADECO President and the very simple and straightforward wording of the letter to present a valid and workable solution to the present problem.

EQ Application

Responding with behaviour that reflects:

- recognition of own and others' emotions
- a match with ethical principles and values
- a relevant communication protocol.

That is why his behaviour illustrates EQ – application. It recognised both his own and the other teams' emotions, particularly recognising that the BAe team's tiredness accentuated their reaction to the news of the crash. Being so close the triumph and then facing the possibility of having it snatched away meant that their advice had to be treated very carefully. Instead of weighing up the likelihood of the LADECO executives having heard of the crash and assessing how they would react, he focused on what was the right thing to do and how best to do it.

Key learning points

Saying that ethical behaviour is always the right way to progress is not as easy at it may sound. What was right in these circumstances? Was it trying to safeguard the thousands of jobs dependent on a substantial order? Was it to ignore third-hand information about the air accident involving the BAe 146-200 series aeroplane? Was it right to put the LADECO President on the spot, so that he had to make a decision based on all this uncertainty? It is possible to make a case for a wide range of possible alternative responses. Ultimately, however, valuing relationships, being open and straightforward, showing respect for others and trusting their judgement is the best way to get them to respect you and trust your judgement. That's what the BAe project team leader did, and achieved a successful commercial outcome as the result of his approach.

121

Case Study 2: Cultural Challenge

'The forces of corporate culture are very strong and hard to recognise, and thus hard to change'
Timothy Gallwey, *'The Inner Game of Work'*

Introduction

A 'seamless transition' was the aspiration of the new senior management team of the service company set up specifically to provide a high quality service solution for a £1billion plus major public sector relocation project due for completion in 2003. The project involved managing the transfer of a range of services from existing sites to a purpose built landmark facility in a new location, whilst enabling the client's core business functions to continue without interruption. Services ranged from management of security, technical infrastructure, accommodation and estates, to cleaning, logistics, catering and reception.

The project included not only complex and extensive technical and operational challenges, but also the recruitment and development of the people needed to provide operational management and service delivery. The new company-wide team put into place consisted of people with previous experience of providing these services as former public sector employees, along with recently recruited managers and staff. A major challenge for the new service company was building a cohesive organisational team from these two groups and developing a corporate-wide culture committed to quality customer service. An additional challenge both technically and culturally, involved the new service company working in close partnership with other leading companies brought together specifically to build the new facility and provide additional services.

While the company involved in the case study has not been identified, the process and outcomes outlined in the story and the key learning points have been verified by the director and senior management team of the organisation involved. What is important to note, is that the company's commitment to developing more effective leadership and teamwork with emotional intelligence as a key element within this, also helped in bringing the application of emotional intelligence to the forefront in telling the story.

To meet the challenges involved, effective leadership and teamwork at all levels were crucial to success. A particular challenge was the former civil service culture familiar to a large number of the people involved, unaccustomed to an emphasis on customer service embracing both internal and external customer demands. The following focuses on the people side of the business and the issues involved in leading and managing cultural change, rather than the technical and operational challenges. The story relates to four groups of people:

1. the senior management team
2. operational management
3. service delivery teams, and
4. the strategic partnership group.

The case study concludes with key learning points achieved from the organisation's development into a successful customer-focused enterprise.

The story

An integrated organisation development programme was designed in 2001 to address the people development challenges identified. This was carried out by an external consultancy working in partnership with the senior team (with major involvement of two key people with significant HR responsibility), along with representation from operational management for relevant parts of the programme. Key elements of this included leadership and team development, both for the senior management team and for operational management teams at department and supervisory levels. A subsequent stage involved customer service training for the wider service delivery staff teams.

The aims of the first stage of the organisation development programme were threefold:

1. to develop a cohesive and united senior management team able to successfully lead the relocation project
2. to develop leadership and management competencies of the operational management teams
3. to ensure a corporate approach that achieved effective integration between the first stage training and development, and the subsequent customer service training planned for the wider staff teams.

A training and development analysis of priorities for operational leadership and management identified a number of key issues for the people involved. These included their uncertainty about the future, lack of clarity of individuals' roles and responsibilities and the need to develop a more customer-focused culture towards the delivery of services to both internal and external customers. Uncertainty about the future included in particular, the threat perceived by the former public sector staff group of the change implications involved and how this would impact on their future roles, responsibilities and job security. Their previously limited experience of leadership and management development also meant there was a general perception of having little need for ongoing learning. (This perception was highlighted by a comment made by one of the operational managers when the development programme was being discussed '*I don't need any more management training, I did mine 20 years ago!'*)

Along with the strategic responsibility of the senior management team, it was recognised that those with operational leadership responsibility had a key role to play in positively influencing and leading their team members towards relocation and resettlement at the new site. Demonstrating full support for the company's vision, mission and values by their behaviour, and facilitating the relevant changes in behaviour needed by people in their teams was crucial to the success of the project.

The senior management team

Effective teamwork within the senior team was seen as essential by them in providing a clear strategic focus and a 'shared leadership' approach. The team also recognised that to achieve optimum teamwork between them and to influence the organisational cultural changes they were seeking, investment in their own training and development demonstrated a 'lead by example' learning commitment to the operational management and staff teams. Despite the work pressures they were under, both team and individual development was subsequently undertaken with a number of stages involved over a period of several months.

The initial stage involved a 'current state' analysis questionnaire completed by all members of the team to assess key areas of the team's effectiveness. These included clarity of strategic direction and organisational objectives, monitoring and evaluation procedures and working relationship, with a specific emphasis on the application of emotional intelligence to both strategic and operational management decisions. While a number of positive attributes were recognised by the team, including clear overall aims and effective service monitoring procedures, a number of key issues that needed to be addressed were also identified. These included:

- the need for an effective and efficient company-wide communication strategy providing a consistent message
- the need to engage more effectively with others and lead by example
- the importance of defining objectives that ensured key measures of success were clarified
- the need to seek more feedback and to listen more.

Open and honest debate on all issues affecting the team's performance and what action was needed to address these in coaching meetings and team workshops helped to develop more effective teamwork. One-to-one coaching meetings also gave individuals the opportunity to focus reflection on their personal contributions to effective teamwork and any development needs within a confidential forum.

Learning themes agreed by the team as a result of their development included:

- recognition of the importance of collective leadership with shared values as a foundation for this
- the need for the team to maintain a strategic focus and address the most important issues as a team
- the importance of building trusting and valued relationships.

The opportunity to value emotional input at work rather than smother it was also highlighted along with what was described by the senior team as *'The power of passion for a common purpose'*. Further learning identified the importance of bringing learning to life and an acknowledgement that they had achieved some significant steps towards becoming a 'Learning Organisation'.

Operational leadership

The overlapping modular development programmes for operational managers covered subject areas and content relevant to the level of leadership and management responsibility involved. These were designed with a focus on key areas of managing change, performance and resources, leadership and team working, plus high quality customer service. Development of both leadership and management competencies were included as a point of reference.

Effective communication and a corporate team approach were integral to the overall organisation development programme, with an emphasis on emotionally intelligent leadership recognised as being fundamental to effective people management and the development of productive working relationships. The principles and practice of the 'Learning Organisation' were encouraged throughout by facilitated learning and influencing participants to take ownership for their performance and continuing development and learning.

A number of the debates during early workshops were however dominated by a small but vociferous minority of individuals, who lost no opportunity in airing their grievances (generally unconnected to the topic in hand), and in aiming to undermine those who wanted to engage in productive debate. Despite this, as the programme progressed and as more groups of managers were involved, there was a marked shift in emphasis towards a majority who were both willing and able to learn and change. Subsequent workshop debates focused primarily on discussing real and practical issues of concern and identifying action plans to deal with these. The confidential forum of one-to-one coaching also helped to facilitate reflective practice discussions and the transfer of learning to the workplace. The commitment demonstrated by members of the senior management team by their active involvement in a number of the workshop debates and their genuine interest in engaging with the groups in open and honest debate provided further positive stimulus towards achieving the desired cultural changes.

As a sequel to the leadership development programmes, the focus then shifted to developing more effective teamwork between operational managers at all levels. A similar process to the senior management team was involved, with a first stage analysis of team effectiveness and facilitation of a series of workshops to address the issues identified that were blocking corporate teamwork and to build on the activities that were supporting this. Issues identified ranged from a perception by a minority of operational managers that the senior team did not listen, to issues relating to practical items such as the lack of some facilities needed to maximise efficient service delivery at the new site.

Service delivery teams

The priority for teams involved in delivering front line services (such as logistics, estates, cleaning, catering, reception etc.), was to provide quality customer service matching (or exceeding) contract agreements for the client. Customer service input on the operational leadership development programmes was designed to provide a framework for their line managers' direct involvement in training and developing their teams. In conjunction with this, a company-wide programme of customer service training for all service teams was designed and delivered. The programme's aim was to increase pride in, and ownership for delivering quality service to both internal and external customers, through commitment to more effective teamwork both within teams and across the company as a whole.

The workshops delivered as part of this programme were co-facilitated by external consultants along with one or more members of senior management. As part of each workshop, a team exercise involved each group devising their proposal for a motto to illustrate the company's commitment to quality customer service. All motto submissions were subsequently put forward for a democratic company-wide vote, with the assurance made by the senior management team that, even if the selected motto may not have been their first choice as an executive team, they would support and formally adopt the popular choice as the official company motto.

Strategic partnerships

After initially working within more formal client/contract arrangements, the concept of working within a partnering/teamwork framework formed the basis of the relationship with the other leading national companies brought together specifically for the new build project. The 'partnering' concept inevitably meant that more emphasis was needed on the building and maintaining of productive working relationships between the people in the organisations involved, with the application of emotional intelligence playing a key part in this development.

Key issues identified at an early stage of 'partnering' working practices included uncertainty of the overall management framework, a lack of clarity regarding roles, responsibilities and working relationships as well as details of business processes and a need for effective teamwork, especially between individuals working within 'Task Teams' across the three companies. Supplementary issues also identified, included the need for clear direction, support and leadership from senior management, and demonstration of commitment from everyone involved in achieving effective partnering relationships (highlighted by a small minority of individuals indicating continued reluctance to support the partnering concept).

A number of workshops and other events (such as social gatherings and outdoor team challenges) were held to address these issues. These were held both leading up to the relocation project deadline and after the move was implemented.

The EQ4U Process Model
The following mapping against the **EQ4U PROCESS MODEL** outlines how each element relates to the groups involved. Key learning points are then summarised and conclusions drawn on the contribution of emotional intelligence to cultural change.

Self-awareness and understanding

- Awareness and acknowledgement of own body language 'signals' and associated emotions
- Understanding own emotions ~ listening to and reflecting on intuitive feelings *(gut reactions)*

Initial response to any personal development proposal is often denial and defensiveness rather than open acknowledgement of need and willingness to learn. Despite this, self-awareness was effectively demonstrated by the senior management team in acknowledging the need to invest in their development, both individually and collectively. While there was some scepticism indicated initially and misgivings about the value of investing in people development (including their own) at a time when operational work pressures were especially demanding, the team indicated a heightened self-awareness by collective agreement that investment was essential both for them and others.

A significant proportion of operational managers demonstrated at an early stage of the programme however, both limited self-awareness and defensiveness towards the need for them to be more effective at leading and managing. A minority of those with supervisory responsibility even took the view that their role was not 'management'. The continuum of views at this early stage ranged from welcoming a development opportunity, through to indifference/acceptance and opposition. The majority fell into the indifference/acceptance group, with a minority appreciative and a small number of individuals actively hostile towards participation in any sort of development programme. The opportunity to voice their feelings and share views in both group forums and confidentially one to one, provided an opportunity for reflection and self-awareness and helped to facilitate understanding of any emotional resistance they had. More open expression of self-awareness and intuitive approaches developed throughout the programme.

The approach of the senior management team was crucial towards both leadership and team development for operational management and customer service training for the wider staff group. Expression of self-awareness through sharing feelings about what the issues were in providing quality customer service and what the personal impact may be on them for addressing these, was actively encouraged in the workshop sessions.

With regard to the working arrangements with other organisations involved, the idea of working within a partnering framework resulted from growing collective self-awareness of the senior management involved that this would be a better and more productive way of working than via more formal contracted client/customer relationships. The initiative was however first led by one director and his team, with support from other senior management in the other organisations subsequently endorsing this approach.

Awareness and understanding of others

- Being interested in and aware of others' body language and behaviours
- Interpreting and anticipating others' emotions within the overall context of the situation

'Awareness of others' for members by the senior management team was especially apparent in making an open commitment to their own development. Because of the reluctance initially expressed by a number of the operational managers to participate in a development programme, it was especially important for the senior team to be exemplars as 'collective leaders' in supporting their own need to learn and change both individually and a team.

'Awareness of others' by operational managers in relation to the senior managers was not immediately or significantly apparent on commencement of their leadership programme, other than a recognition expressed by some of the individuals involved that there was a need for change. 'Other-awareness' in a small number of cases, related more to listening to the views of some of their colleagues (who were former public sector employees), who felt aggrieved that they had lost previous employee rights perceived as preferable to those within their new contracts. For their line managers to support the company by welcoming participation in the programme was therefore seen as 'disloyal'. (Emphasis needs to be made that this resistance related to only a small minority within the overall group.) As with the self-awareness factor and the impact of this on others, 'other-awareness' became more apparent as the programme progressed and more productive working relationships developed between the group as a whole.

'Other-awareness' for the staff groups involved in the customer service training related to a number of others including their peers and line managers. Particular emphasis was however on an awareness of senior managers' expectations, in particular how the services provided by the company matched or exceeded contract agreements with the client. Senior management representation and participation in all the workshops involved, provided the opportunity for effective dialogue and open and honest feedback and better understanding between the groups and individuals involved.

With regard to the 'partnering' initiative, this required a genuine effort from all the parties involved in having more awareness and understanding of others. Getting to know each other through the series of events aimed at building better relationships as well as more efficient working practices (and especially the outdoor team challenge event), helped to support this.

Reflection

Reflection on:

- an ethical framework of principles and values.
- the overall situational context including own and others' circumstances.
- own emotions and others' anticipated emotions.
- communication that will:
  ⇨ demonstrate recognition and understanding of the context;
  ⇨ be clearly and appropriately communicated;
  ⇨ be genuine, open and honest; and
  ⇨ show an appropriate degree of warmth

The senior management team's reflection focus throughout was on aiming to achieve the company's vision and strategic objectives through the practice of their stated values, underpinned by the company charter which defined commitments and expectations of all stakeholders. The values and charter statements therefore provided the framework by which performance and behaviour of everyone in the company could be judged. These included a commitment to an open and honest culture, corporate teamwork and effective communication.

Their own development as an effective senior management team with demonstration of a 'shared leadership' commitment through 'walking the talk' was recognised as essential for the overall success of the organisation's development. Working towards becoming an effective 'Learning Organisation' and how this could be practiced was a key topic of debate, in both group and one to one coaching discussions.

For operational managers, workshop debates throughout the development programmes reflected on the match with the company's values and charter and how these related to their leadership and management performance. While there were a number of challenging issues to debate about putting principles into practice (and heated discussions about these!), recognition of the genuine commitment demonstrated by senior management was reinforced as the organisation development programme progressed and there was wider management and staff awareness.

As with senior and operational management, customer service training for the service delivery teams was underpinned by the company's values and charter. Referring back to these as a frame of reference helped to focus discussions on the principles involved, especially those relating to internal and external customer service and the rights, responsibilities and expectations allied to these. Senior management commitment to listening to and involving staff (and putting the principles into practice!), was aptly demonstrated by involving all staff in drafting proposals for the company's customer service 'motto'.

The framework of principles and values of the strategic partnership between the three organisations involved was effectively demonstrated by their express commitment to sign up to their 'Partnering Charter'. Charter statements emphasised commitments such as working together as one mutually supportive team, constantly striving to improve, showing respect, honesty, trust and openness, recognising others' efforts and achievements, communicating effectively, and commitment to success whilst recognising the interests of all stakeholders.

EQ Application

Responding with behaviour that reflects:

- recognition of own and others' emotions
- a match with ethical principles and values
- a relevant communication protocol.

While there were a number of challenges that had to be faced in developing more effective leadership and teamwork, what was also clear as the programme developed was a positive shift in perception by the operational managers who were crucial in influencing their teams towards achieving this. Behaviour reflecting more self and other awareness and more effective and value based communication was demonstrated by the feedback received from the managers concerned, with even the majority of those who had initially voiced their opposition actively endorsing the benefits achieved.

Evidence of the changes achieved included feedback noting that communication across the company was 'much better', more feeling of being part of a wider company team as well as better teamwork within departments, plus more confidence in dealing with change and in helping their teams to deal with this. A specific communication improvement noted were the company's core briefing sessions now being more of a two way process (and more effective listening from management) with feedback and ideas encouraged from staff.

Inspiration to take learning to the workplace was also mentioned, with one group of managers producing of their own volition, a well thought out and detailed proposal of action they could take to lead change both within and across their departments. Their proposal entitled 'Changes' was formally presented to the senior management team, with accompanying slide show imaginatively illustrating the change perspective, with visions of trees and their seasonal changes in the introduction to this.

The foundation for the changes described was the senior

management team's demonstration of commitment to put into practice the principles espoused within the company's values and charter statements. The result was growing understanding, trust and commitment between the various teams and individuals involved, and the development of a more open and supportive 'corporate team' culture. The motto chosen by the staff, 'Committed to Excellence', was formally adopted and incorporated into the company's own charter statement. The business continues to build its commercial success by exceeding customer expectations through a more cohesive organisational team culture committed to service excellence.

The organisations involved in the strategic alliance intend to maintain a partnership approach for the remaining years of the business agreement between them. The 'Partnering Charter', and in particular the development of emotionally intelligent productive working relationships, was the first stage in this approach. The people involved continue to work towards its achievement.

Key learning points

- Commitment and a shared leadership approach from management at all levels and from the senior management team in particular is essential to success.
- Clarification, communication and, most importantly, application of vision and values by appropriate behaviour are necessary foundations for cultural change. This applies especially by those in leadership roles.
- Everyone at every level and in every function needs to have a sense of ownership and feel involved in contributing towards achieving the organisation's vision. Welcoming ideas and ensuring there is a forum to facilitate this, effective two way feedback and a valued reward system help to achieve this.
- Despite significant commitment, investment and effort a minority of individuals have mind sets unwilling to adapt to change. Indeed, a small minority (and even one individual) can have a disproportionate and damaging influence on others' approach and

behaviour and the 'sub culture' within his/her department. This influence is damaging at either management or service level, but especially so if the individual/s concerned are working in a leadership /supervisory role.

- The converse of the above point is also true, i.e. the 'contagion effect' also applies in a positive way through the power of collective leadership, teamwork and the influence of individuals on others.
- Sustained and focused investment which recognises the needs of individuals and groups is needed to maintain and develop the productive relationships important for continued success.
- While some 'quick wins' can be achieved by timely, appropriate (and emotionally intelligent!) actions, there is no 'quick fix' to cultural change.

Conclusions

It was clear from the beginning that important cultural issues needed to be addressed if the desired changes in approach and behaviour were to be realised. It would nevertheless be naive to suggest that because emotional intelligence was openly recognised as a key component of the organisation development process that all the leadership and teamwork issues were fully resolved. Emotional intelligence and open debate about how applied EQ contributes to building productive working relationships, undoubtedly made a significant difference however, in both identifying issues blocking effective leadership and teamwork and in developing action plans to deal with these. A range of important benefits were therefore achieved, relating not only to the individuals and groups involved but also the company as a whole.

While EQ was an important part of the process for everyone concerned, the group for whom it was most important was the senior management team. Without their genuine commitment to authenticity by 'walking the talk' and demonstrating in practice the behaviours that showed this adherence to company values, the cultural shift would not have occurred; the most important of these being an ongoing commitment to learning and change.

Case Study 3: Teams Need Trust

'Trust men and they will be true to you; treat them greatly, and they will show themselves great.'

Ralph Waldo Emerson
19th century American poet and essayist

Introduction

This is a story of a struggling, medium-sized business, part of a much larger multinational, where the management team brought about significant changes in the way the business was run and made it into a successful and thriving concern. They did it largely by:

- trusting the mainly unskilled and semi-skilled workforce to take an active role in managing the business on a day-to-day basis
- designing and making significant improvements in production processes
- monitoring output quality and volumes
- looking after their own machinery and workspaces.

The packaging business is one of the most competitive there is, particularly when supplying businesses in the food and personal care industry. Food processors and toiletry products manufacturers, the customers of the packaging businesses, are under enormous price pressure from the big retailers, which are themselves engaged in fiercely price-competitive battles with each other. So this price competition gets pushed back down the supply chain.

What's more, food, grocery and toiletries packaging is all about large volumes, but with precision printing done under strict food hygiene conditions. The precision reflects the importance of packaging in selling products off the shelves. Faced with a wide choice of products, it's the packaging which often causes customers to choose one brand in preference to another. In this highly price-sensitive, high volume, low margin industry, companies live a precarious life. One such was Lawson Mardon Packaging, bought by Alusuisse, which then merged its plastics packaging operations with another subsidiary, Fibrenyle. Alusuisse was then in turn taken over by Alcan, and Fibrenyle was subsequently sold to another European packaging business, Polimoon.

Despite this relentless change of ownership, itself a destabilising experience, the Lawson Mardon Plastics (now Fibrenyle) factory at Sutton-in-Ashfield, in the extreme west of Nottinghamshire, managed to undertake a quiet revolution in the way that it operated, a revolution that was based on managers trusting their workforce to take responsibility for large parts of the day-to-day control of operations.

The story

A new management team had joined Lawson Mardon Plastics in 1991 with a brief to turn the company round. Steve Isherwood, then Operations Director and subsequently MD of the Fibrenyle business in the UK, introduced organisational strategies which put team working at the heart of the company's operations, prompted by the problems the company faced in satisfying customer demands for improvements in performance.

The company produced a wide range of plastic products used in food packaging, including coffee jar caps, denture cleaning tablet packs and widgets – the devices used in beer cans to create the same effect as draught beer when the cans are opened. Their factory floor workforce ranged from highly trained printers and maintenance technicians to semi-skilled machine operators, many with little or no formal training or qualifications.

Their problems combined difficulties in achieving the quality standards required by customers, difficulties in meeting delivery schedules, and difficulties in keeping costs down to the level needed to remain competitive. To address these, the management team started out by creating a number of Cross Functional Teams (CFTs) to examine the core problems facing the company, drawing on the knowledge and skills of employees from all areas and at all levels in the company.

The principle behind CFTs was that all the people involved in the production of products – from the purchasing people buying raw materials to the sales people dealing with customers, via the shop floor workers and technical support staff – needed to work collaboratively, in a structured way, to work out why things were going wrong and how best to put them right. Underpinning this was the simple matter of trust – that the management trusted their employees to know better than them what was wrong and how to put it right.

This improvement process led the production employees to develop team-working within Cells, each Cell being staffed by three teams working eight hour shifts. Traditionally, production was organised around functions – plastic moulding, printing, etc. - with a product moving from one functional activity to another. Cell working joins together several functional processes – in many cases physically joins them together by feeding the output of one machine directly into another. This demands multi-skilled teams, rather than having teams of plastic moulding or printing specialists.

One consequence of this approach is that stock of work-in-progress is reduced or eliminated. There are exceptions, of course. One was on the widget line, for example, because it required so many plastic moulding machines to feed the nitrogen injection machine that this could only be managed by building stock. Even so, there was never more than a few hours stock of work in progress at any one time, minimising working capital.

Since the production process relied mainly on raw feedstock for the plastic moulding machines, and the products are supplied directly to customers soon after they are produced, the company is able to operate a Just In Time (JIT) system, producing products for delivery to customers' own production lines as and when they are needed. Cell working does not in itself require a team-based approach, but it creates a physical and organisational environment in which it is possible. The lack of a buffer of work in progress creates a significant degree of inter-dependence between the various elements of any production process. If one machine breaks down, or one person is off sick, the whole process may go down. For this reason, Lawson Mardon also operates three other critical elements in their organisational structure:

- Training, to raise skills and create multi-skilling – the company encourages all its employees to achieve NVQs in relevant skill areas
- Total Quality Management (TQM)
- Total Productive Maintenance (TPM).

Higher skill levels mean that machinery is used properly, improving quality and reducing downtime for operator faults. Multi-skilling allows fewer employees to operate in a cell, reducing dependence on a limited number of specialists and enabling individuals to cover for each other's absences. This training is shared between a specialist training manager and the Team Leader, who coaches fellow team members.

TQM is reflected in the strong customer-focus and continuous improvement using Statistical Process Control (SPC), Pareto Analysis, and Cause and Effect Diagrams with Action Cards (CEDAC – a variant on the Ishikawa or fishbone diagrams that constitute one of the seven tools of quality improvement developed by Japanese quality guru Dr Kaoru Ishikawa). The company encouraged cell teams to deal directly with their opposite numbers on the assembly lines of their customers, identifying and resolving problems through their own expertise and the technical advice of engineers and others.

TPM emphasises preventive maintenance to minimise breakdowns, placing the responsibility on operators to maintain and monitor the performance of the machinery they used. They were responsible for Overall Equipment Efficiency (OEE), which combined machine availability, machine efficiency and product quality. Current performance data is constantly displayed in the cell and team meetings can be convened easily to address problems as soon as they are identified.

Team-working at Lawson Mardon Plastics can be seen as being one part of a complex of strategies designed to achieve corporate objectives. Team members spontaneously talk about corporate profitability, customer satisfaction and production efficiency because they understand the relationships and share managers' understanding of them. Unskilled or semi-skilled machine operators are trained to maintain their own equipment and make simple repairs and adjustments that previously required skilled fitters. Skilled people are encouraged to share their skills. Under-performing team members are encouraged by fellow team members to resolve their problems, as they are seen as letting down the team by their behaviour.

The EQ4U Process Model

There are many features of the Lawson Mardon Plastics/Fibrenyle story that would place it firmly in the TQM/Business Process Engineering story and there it would lie. However, such an analysis would fail to recognise the underpinning issues of leadership, trust and emotional intelligence that made the whole revolution in management and operations possible.

Self-awareness and understanding

- Awareness and acknowledgement of own body language 'signals' and associated emotions
- Understanding own emotions ~ listening to and reflecting on intuitive feelings *(gut reactions)*

For Steve Isherwood and his management team, the starting point was to recognise that the potential of a large part of the workforce was being largely ignored. As John Revill, a team leader in one production cell commented, 'It was as if, when you came to work in the morning, you left your brain in a box by the door'. Steve and his colleagues believed that their workforce had far more ability than they had been credited with and that if they were given the opportunity to take on more responsibility they would use it well.

The trust that the managers showed in their employees was shown to have been well founded, but at first that's all there was, trust. They had to believe in their gut feelings that, given the chance, the employees were capable of doing far more than they had been trusted to do in the past.

Awareness and understanding of others

- Being interested in and aware of others' body language and behaviours
- Interpreting and anticipating others' emotions within the overall context of the situation

This meant that they had to think through the implications of what they were asking shop floor workers to do. Some were gaining new responsibilities whilst others might well feel that they were reducing theirs. If maintenance fitters were training production workers to do their jobs, what would happen to those jobs? When skilled printers were training machine operators in the complexities of printing, were they deskilling their jobs?

The management team recognised that they were asking people to take risks and to trust them that the end result would be a more challenging and yet worthwhile job. There were financial rewards for all employees, in the way of bonuses to reflect the financial position of the company, and also higher pay for those unskilled operatives who acquired new skills. There was a lot of planning and discussion with all those affected by the changes, and their union representatives, because the managers recognised the fears, doubts and uncertainties

143

that their proposals represented. They also introduced progressively, to allow those affected to see some benefits from the new way of working, before progressing further.

Reflection

Reflection on:

- an ethical framework of principles and values.
- the overall situational context including own and others' circumstances.
- own emotions and others' anticipated emotions.
- communication that will:
  ⇨ demonstrate recognition and understanding of the context;
  ⇨ be clearly and appropriately communicated;
  ⇨ be genuine, open and honest; and
  ⇨ show an appropriate degree of warmth

This recognition of the feelings of everyone involved and the change that it mean for them, in terms of their job role and position, was matched by a clear policy of communication and consultation. By ensuring that the purpose of the changes were made clear and that the principles underpinning them were overt, the company was able to build up trust and commitment in a workplace that had been characterised previously by a very 'command and control' managerial environment. The commitment to change was reinforced by the investment in training and qualifications, so that employees could see that they were accruing a benefit that would stand them in good stead. As one employee commented, *'I can now get a job far more easily than I could before. The difference now is that I don't want to!'*

EQ Application

Responding with behaviour that reflects:

- recognition of own and others' emotions
- a match with ethical principles and values
- a relevant communication protocol.

The commitment to the principles that underpinned the new approach to quality was clear. When a customer was having problems with supplied product, it was the Cell team that went out to Germany to discuss the problem with their counterparts. This was a public statement of trust in the workforce to be able to solve problems themselves, with managers and technical experts available as consultants to the team, not as controllers. The truth of the management team's commitment to the values and principles they claimed is reinforced every time they show that trust in their employees, and would be destroyed if they were to revert to traditional management approach just once.

This is where emotionally competent leadership is apparent, when leaders demonstrate their respect for others through their behaviour. People respond emotionally to the behaviour of others, especially when it comes to trust. Trust is a precious commodity, hard to acquire and easy to lose. The true test of trust is how someone behaves when things go wrong. It is easy to trust people when everything is going smoothly, but the leader who adopts an autocratic, top-down approach when problems arise is the leader who has forfeited any chance of retaining trust in the future.

Key learning points

This case study, similar in some ways to the fifth case study, *Getting the engaged tone*, proves that people are capable of doing far more than we often credit them with, if only we are willing to trust them. By having that trust, and a vision of an organisation that was capable of responding directly to the needs of its customers, the company was able to bring about massive change in its processes and ways of working.

One of the features of the way the business operates is its constant striving for improvement through innovation, and its faith in the workforce as being able to develop and introduce creative ideas. What's more, by allowing teams to make many of the day-to-day decisions affecting their own work areas and allowing them some control over their own working environment, they have reduced the pressure on managers, allowing them to focus on more strategic issues.

This case study illustrates many of the key ideas that we have been emphasising in **MINDCHANGE**, ideas like the importance of two-way trust and respect in leadership, the ability of ordinary people to be creative, and the vast potential that all of us have, if only it is recognised.

Case Study 4:
Change Is About Listening

*'A fool thinks he needs no advice,
but a wise man listens to others.'*
Book of Proverbs Ch.12, v.15

Introduction

What happens when your newest customer, a customer you feel
privileged to have buying from you turns round and says, *'Actually,
you're not very good, it's just that all the competitors were even
worse?'* How do you respond to such a damning indictment, one that
says that the customer is only buying from you until they can find
someone better?

That was the situation facing WH Smith & Sons (Tools) Ltd, or
WHS as they tend to call themselves. They had won a contract to
produce leather covered gear knobs for Nissan in the early 1990s, a
few years after the car company first set up in the UK. Now they were
being told that they were only just clinging on to the contract with
their teeth and had to work hard to keep it. For Colin Sarson, the
company's MD, this was a wake-up call that led to a major change in
his approach to leadership and management, a change that involved
him in developing his and other managers' emotional intelligence.
The result was a remarkable success story in British manufacturing.

The story

According to an article by Judith Kenner Thompson and Robert

Rehder in *Business Horizons* (Jan-Feb 1995: Nissan U.K.: a worker's paradox?):

'There are currently 132 British companies supplying parts and components to Nissan Motors UK. Company engineers have worked closely with local companies to specify what is needed and bring quality standards up to those demanded by NMUK..... Nissan has helped suppliers develop their R&D skills in-house. This has resulted in essential quality improvements and cost reductions in the Nissan manufacturing chain by providing both essential lean system training and long-term contracts that call for step-by-step price reductions and quality improvement. These key lean system tenets, adapted and refined in the U.S., have also served as important building blocks at NMUK.'

For WHS this was something completely new. The company was started in the 1930s by a toolmaker (WH Smith – no relation to the newsagents!), working in his garden shed. When his son Fred joined the company he expanded the business from making tools into injection moulding with those same tools, and to this was added sub-assembly of the moulded components which offered customers a one-stop-shop if they wanted it, from tool manufacture to assembled product. What Nissan said was that this innovative and successful expansion had been just enough to get them accepted as a supplier. Now they had to work hard to maintain that position.

Colin Sarson has spent his working life at WHS, including working there before he left school, during his summer holidays. The company is still family owned and Colin has moved up through the company to be the Managing Director, with Fred's son as Chairman. He describes the stunned feeling they had after their first Supplier Development Audit from Nissan, walking away with their 'chins on the floor'. He realised then that he had fallen into a classic time management failing and had been confusing 'busyness' with 'effectiveness'. By spending so much of his time in meetings and constantly rushing from place to place, he had avoided spending time actually talking to, and much less listening to and understanding the people he led.

The audit led the management team to look both long and hard at themselves and at best practice elsewhere in three key areas:

1. in their use of technology
2. in the way they treated their people
3. at their training.

The result was that the management team realised they needed a fundamental change in the culture of the organisation, that it had to be led from the top and that it had to start by asking people for their ideas and listening to them. If they wanted their employees to make a real contribution to the development of the business, they had to start by finding out what they were capable of contributing and what it was their staff wanted in return.

Surprisingly enough, the things that really concerned people were very basic. They wanted a work environment that was pleasant and comfortable. What they didn't want was the large puddles in the car park, dirty toilets and so much noise they couldn't hear each other speak! None of this was very difficult to deliver and yet the effect of creating a more pleasant environment was dramatic. It made coming to work less unpleasant and more importantly, showed that the managers could actually listen to people. A refurbishment of the factory made it into a far more attractive place to work, and the introduction of a one hour per week training entitlement for all staff showed that the company was serious about its commitment to supporting and enabling its staff to develop themselves. As Colin Sarson says:

'The business needed change, the customers were getting more demanding. But how do we motivate the man at midnight, working the night shift? We talk to him in the middle of the night. What's more, we go and talk to him in his workplace. I had to force myself to allocate time to do what initially seemed to be a wasteful activity, walking round the factory meeting people and talking to them. It's only then that people become motivated. Managers and supervisors realised that if they communicate with their staff in the right way they would deliver the quality. They should be there to support staff in delivering what customers want.'

Colin Sarson goes on to describe what, for him, are the qualities of a good manager. *'They have to think of themselves, motivate themselves to improve and develop their own performance. Then they have to be caring and considerate of the people around them. They should spend half their time helping to improve themselves, and half helping others to improve.'*

One example in the WHS factory illustrates this principle well. WHS supply moulding to Triton, the leading shower manufacturer. They replaced several other suppliers, and moved from packing parts into cardboard boxes to using standard reusable plastic cartons on pallets. These are delivered to the Triton factory and act as a simple but effective stock control system, known as Kanban. (Kanban is a Japanese word meaning 'signal'. It is one of the tools used in a Just In Time system, triggering re-supply to keep production going.)

The WHS driver monitors the level of stock at the Triton factory and uses a mobile phone to alert the production cell (the team responsible for producing the Triton components). The production team then produces the items needed whilst the driver makes the two-hour journey back to the WHS factory, collects the items and takes them to Triton. There are no production schedules and there is no management involvement. The process is driven by the cells and the driver, who record what they supply and keep the production controllers informed.

Each cell is responsible for taking the company's objectives and translating them into their particular aspect of the organisation. The production team then display these objectives and the activities needed to achieve them on the notice boards in their cell and then monitor their own performance. The enabling role of managers, the training entitlement and the 24/7 Learning Centre, are the support mechanism that WHS has put in place to enable the change to happen. As Colin Sarson says:

'The opportunities are endless. It's possible to go on improving every facet of the business. We've only really just started.'

The EQ4U Process Model

Although it's easy to see the change at WHS as primarily being about systems and procedures, the reality is very different. The changes that took place in the way that the company operated were a direct consequence of changes in the behaviour of the managers in the way people were treated. This change in approach clearly reflects the significance and value of emotionally intelligent behaviour and the part this plays in building more productive working relationships.

Self-awareness and understanding

- Awareness and acknowledgement of own body language 'signals' and associated emotions
- Understanding own emotions ~ listening to and reflecting on intuitive feelings *(gut reactions)*

The biggest challenge for Colin Sarson was to realise that he wasn't wasting his time when he started walking round the factory just talking to people. He had to be aware of what his body language had been saying. The rushing around, the continual meetings, the general distance between him and the shop floor said loud and clear that he was too important for them to speak to, and suggested that they were far too unimportant for him to waste his time with them. But if he was to change that behaviour, he had to change his own thinking and attitudes and listen to his own emotions. It's not enough to say, 'I should spend more time talking to people' - you have to actually believe that you should and want to hear what people had to say. That was the first stage in the process of the steep learning curve he and his management team had to climb.

151

Awareness and understanding of others

- Being interested in and aware of others' body language and behaviours
- Interpreting and anticipating others' emotions within the overall context of the situation

---

Listening to people, really 'listening to understand' rather than just to respond, is the hardest part of communication. The management team also had to learn to listen, and to recognise what people were saying to them through all aspects of their communication and not just via the words they used. They also had to be prepared to recognise that, by asking people what they wanted, they had raised expectations that they would be listened to and their requests acted on. Not doing anything about the car parks and the toilets before they were asked for their ideas was just irritating to employees. Not doing anything after they had asked for ideas was insulting.

One of the reasons that many managers don't like asking questions is that they are afraid of the answers. Asking people for their opinion raises their expectations that they will be listened to, and raising expectations was what WHS was doing. However, they were aware of the emotional response if they did nothing, and therefore made a commitment to take action and to do so as quickly as they could. The management team recognised that it wasn't tarmac on the car park or clean loos that motivated people, but the recognition that they actually cared about their concerns. Motivation is a purely emotional response to the world about us, the way that we relate to it and the way it relates to us. As leaders and managers they were able to provide people with the conditions for motivation, the motivation itself comes from within the individual at a personal level.

Reflection

Reflection on:

- an ethical framework of principles and values.
- the overall situational context including own and others' circumstances.
- own emotions and others' anticipated emotions.
- communication that will:
  ⇨ demonstrate recognition and understanding of the context;
  ⇨ be clearly and appropriately communicated;
  ⇨ be genuine, open and honest; and
  ⇨ show an appropriate degree of warmth

What Colin Sarson also recognised was that it was no use talking about what was important, he had to live up to the principles and values that he espoused. He has a small office that is virtually empty. He doesn't need much space because he's hardly ever there. If he wants to meet people he goes to their workspace.

The company recognised that people had to have better skills and so they instituted the one-hour per week entitlement to job-related training and created the facility to deliver it. Like Colin himself, they prefer to develop and grow their own talent to demonstrate they value their own people.

This type of commitment comes from constant self-examination and reflection on individuals' own performance and how this affects the performance of the organisation as a whole. It is demonstrated by the regular reviews that all employees have with their managers, to encourage them to look at their own performance and identify what development they need. It also comes from the company's commitment to external assessment and to self-analysis, for ISO 9000, ISO 14001, Investors in People and Investors in Excellence. This public commitment to constant reflection and self-assessment creates a culture within the organisation that encourages open communication, honesty and, despite its size, a real sense of common identity and shared responsibility.

EQ Application

Responding with behaviour that reflects:

- recognition of own and others' emotions
- a match with ethical principles and values
- a relevant communication protocol.

The WHS story is inspiring because the company is so down to earth. It is involved in all aspects of the production process, from the high skills and high-tech tool-making end (the company invests heavily in up to date machinery to be able to compete with the best) to the low skilled assembly of components (where it has also invested in robotics to maintain its competitiveness). But what makes it successful, alongside the technical superiority it strives to maintain, is the people it employs. By treating people as important, acknowledging that how they feel about their work and their employer is as important – if not more important – than the tasks they are performing, it has recognised the importance of emotions in enabling change to take place.

By living up to the principles and values it proclaims, in the way that it values its employees and invests in them, and in the way that it emphasises direct, personal communication, it has transformed the business. What Colin Sarson recognised is that it wasn't easy. Managers had to relearn their way of thinking and behaving. They had to release control and trust people to live up their potential. Above all, they had to spend time listening to people and doing what was asked of them, instead of expecting to tell others what they should do. That requires a high level of emotional intelligence.

Key learning points

- Reflection involves a willingness to be honest with yourself and accept the implications of what you learn about yourself. If you have to change your behaviour to bring about changes in others, you need to reach deep into yourself to accept that this is necessary to overcome what are predominantly emotional barriers to change.

- Change doesn't come easily, but it does come if you truly want it to happen. Managers have to lead change by example, to trust the people who do the work, to know what is best and to be willing to listen to them and act on their suggestions.

- Trust is an emotional response to other people's behaviour. It is hard to earn and easy to lose. To engender trust, managers have to start out by trusting. Showing trust in others creates the emotional climate within which people will start trusting their managers.

- Significant change is often started by external forces, like the Nissan Audit at WHS. The hardest part is to maintain the momentum without these external pressures, creating them for yourself. Constantly seeking out new challenges isn't easy, and yet a company like WHS has managed to achieve its competitive edge by not settling back on the laurels of past success. True leadership comes from being able to set goals for yourself and others that stretch people and organisations, whilst creating the conditions that make people aspire to achieve them.

Case Study 5:
Getting the Engaged Tone

'Tell people what your dream is and what it might mean for them, and then convince them it's worth it for them to help you get there.'
Patricia Vaz, first Director of BT Payphones
and Businesswoman of the Year, 1994

Introduction

This is very much a story of building triumph from adversity, of the importance of effective leadership, good management and, above all, of emotional intelligence in action. It's also about engaging the workforce in achieving goals that seem both unrealistic and, at times, threatening, and still being able to win through.

Since the 1990s, when this story is largely set, the growth of mobile phones has meant that the BT Payphone business, especially the public call boxes, has suffered severely, although new services (like Internet and email access at railway stations and airports), have helped to keep the business going.

The story

Back in 1988, BT was under fire. Recently privatised, the company was not well loved, particularly its payphone operations. This was before mobile phones had really taken off, but they were gradually encroaching on the payphone business which was already facing competition from other suppliers. More significantly, 30% of all payphones were out of action at any one time, nearer 50% in parts of London and this, BT's public face, was seen as dragging the whole image of the company down. Mike Bett, the MD, had made a commitment on Radio 4's Woman's Hour to achieve 90% serviceability in six months, by 1st April 1989 (April Fools' Day, as many reminded him!). It was this overwhelming challenge that the Payphones division had to live up to.

It was made harder by the fact that nobody had direct responsibility for payphones, and they tended to be at the end of the line when it came to priorities for repair. The solution to this was to create a new business unit responsible for the whole BT payphone operation in the UK. It was created by taking people from the other operating areas, but that was a good opportunity for them to get rid of people they didn't want or need. So the division started very much as the runt of the BT litter. This was the challenge faced by Patricia Vaz, the first Director, appointed in 1992.

Vaz needed to weld a successful business out of the mix of people that she had been given and to engage them with the goals of the business. The primary goal was to maintain and then raise the levels of serviceability that had been achieved by the concerted efforts started back in 1988. One unexpected consequence of getting the phones working and boxes in a decent condition had been that people used them more. Using a payphone was often an impulse purchase, people made calls if they saw a payphone – it reminded them that they needed to ring someone. By increasing the number of payphones, especially in pubs and other places where people gathered, they could increase their turnover.

But that depended on the commitment of the people selling them, installing them, servicing and repairing them, and that was what Patricia Vaz was good at, winning their commitment. She understood that many of them felt disheartened by the move to the Payphones division; it was like being demoted from the premier league to the Football Conference!

The key to the creation of a successful business was the recognition by Patricia Vaz that she needed to communicate with the people working for BT Payphones. She developed her vision of what a successful business would be and a strategy to achieve it. This was communicated to the whole workforce, who were asked to be involved in deciding how it was to be implemented. This involvement was the key, because is showed people that they were valued. Her successor as Director, Bob Warner, was able to use this commitment that she had built up when, in the mid-nineties, he was faced with having to reduce the number of people working in the division to make it cost effective. He was able to do this by drawing on the workforce to find ways of changing working practices to become more efficient, encouraging people to make their own suggestions and strive for economies to enable the business to succeed.

At the end of the nineties, the third Director of BT Payphones, Malcolm Newing, continued this strong emphasis on communication. He and other senior managers regularly telephoned staff in the division to ask them for their feedback on the way that the business was operating. This was designed to do two things, to enable managers to keep in close touch with what was happening on the ground, and to show the employees that their involvement was valued.

By now the division was starting to feel the effects of the growth of mobile phones. To cope with this, they developed new products, payphones offering Internet and email facilities, located at stations, airports and other sites around the country. They had set themselves what Newing calls 'big, hairy, audacious goals' but the confidence of the staff was such that these were seen as being achievable. The growth in confidence from the division that nobody wanted to be part of, to one that was innovative and committed to business success was the direct result of the emphasis that managers had placed on people, what Malcolm Newing describes being 'coaches not cops'.

The EQ4U Process Model
The BT Payphones example demonstrates how emotional intelligence, even if it isn't called that or recognised as such, is the key to implementing a successful strategy, and especially if it's one that involves making fundamental changes in the way people work.

Self-awareness and understanding

- Awareness and acknowledgement of own body language 'signals' and associated emotions
- Understanding own emotions ~ listening to and reflecting on intuitive feelings *(gut reactions)*

In 1994 Patricia Vaz was named Businesswoman of the Year for her work in creating the BT Payphones business. She was acutely aware of the scale of the task that she took on and is frank in admitting that it was a scary task. She knew that she had to demonstrate to everyone in the business her own commitment to the success of the business, but also that she needed their help to make it happen.

By recognising her own feelings about the scale of the tasks she was able to appreciate how everyone else was feeling in the business. This empathy was something that those who had worked for her readily recognised, and it helped to create the sense of belonging that was so significant in the first two years in creating the successful new business unit.

Awareness and understanding of others

- Being interested in and aware of others' body language and behaviours
- Interpreting and anticipating others' emotions within the overall context of the situation

The emphasis on coaching which later developed in the business was done precisely because of the need to build up confidence and commitment further. The senior managers were all trained first of all, and then middle and first line managers, on the basis that it was managers' primary responsibility to develop those that they managed.

159

The emphasis of the coaching programme was on understanding others' needs, goals and concerns, and the barriers that prevented them from progressing. By investing heavily in developing managers, the division wanted to make them more aware of the behaviour of the people they managed and more alert to their feelings.

Reflection

Reflection on:

● an ethical framework of principles and values.
● the overall situational context including own and others' circumstances.
● own emotions and others' anticipated emotions.
● communication that will:
  ⇨ demonstrate recognition and understanding of the context;
  ⇨ be clearly and appropriately communicated;
  ⇨ be genuine, open and honest; and
  ⇨ show an appropriate degree of warmth

Not surprisingly, given that it's a telecommunications business, communication was seen as being central to the development of BT Payphones. But there was a significant problem, a sizeable proportion of the employees were out in vans, on their own, repairing and maintaining payphones. Although newsletters and weekly team meetings were also used, the challenge was for senior managers to communicate directly with the 2,400 staff. It was for this reason that a policy of phoning people regularly was started. The senior management team would aim to speak to as many people as they could, as often as they could, by phoning them in the office or out in their vans. This means that they could obtain information and explain what was happening and why. It also sent out a clear message about the principles and values of the business, that the people who were delivering the service were valued and that their voice needed to be heard.

This strategy reflected Marshall McLuhan's 'the medium is the message'. It was less important what was communicated in these calls, but that they were made. By keeping in contact with the employees on a personal level, even if only occasionally, the message that they were important and their views counted was clear.

EQ Application

Responding with behaviour that reflects:

- recognition of own and others' emotions
- a match with ethical principles and values
- a relevant communication protocol.

The strategy that Patricia Vaz had started which was then followed through by her successors, meant that for some years BT Payphones was the only profitable payphones business in Europe, and led to the division taking over the running of other services, such as the payphones on Dutch railway stations. The BT Payphones strategy was a clear case of applied EQ. This started with the initial recognition that people felt rejected by the rest of the business, because they were involved in the division that was seen as dragging down the whole image of the company. It was followed by seeing that the only way to build the division was by engaging people and getting them committed to Patricia Vaz's 'dream'. It continued in the way that managers took on the primary role of coaches to ensure that they could work with the people they managed to help them develop and improve as the key to developing and improving the business.

Key learning points

This is a story about trust (again) and openness – trust in the people who were expected to turn the business around and openness about the challenges and goals of the business. Most people who came together to form the new operation felt that they were there as a punishment rather than a reward; not a healthy start to a new business. But Patricia Vaz and her successors understood these feelings and set out to work with them, not against them. This was used to advantage, because the sense of adversity that they felt was channelled into meeting the tough targets they were set, a feeling that they would – and could – prove everybody wrong!

In a large organisation it is hard to communicate clearly and effectively, but that is something a telecommunications company should be able to do – if they can't, who can? By setting up strong, effective and two-way communication channels, the managers and leaders were able to make their vision clear to all employees and at the same time to learn about the barriers that were preventing that vision from being realised. This commitment to communicating is very strong and was instrumental in enabling the company to achieve so much against the odds.

Reflections Explored
Part 4:
Developing EQ Leadership

Developing EQ Leadership

'It is by striving ceaselessly to change our emotions that we will succeed in changing our temperament.'
Matthieu Ricard
French philosopher, Buddhist monk and author

So, how do you go about developing your EQ? It's like the woman who asked a New York policeman, *'How do I get to Carnegie Hall?'* His reply? - *'Practice lady, practice!'*

The essence of developing emotional intelligence is reflective practice. It's about conscious and focused thinking relating to your emotions, the emotions of others and the values that guide you, before taking action. While this may sound simple in theory, our instincts, personality and behaviour traits, and our failings as human beings, mean it can often be enormously challenging to put into practice.

Part 4 of **MINDCHANGE** is a guide to how you can develop your EQ by a studied awareness of what's involved in the approach and behaviours of being more emotionally intelligent and in the way that you perform your leadership role. We start with a reminder of the **EQ4U** four stages and the three 'traffic light' elements of the process introduced in Part 1 (emphasising the cyclical procedure involved), then go on to look at each element in turn. The first 'red awareness' element, focuses on aspects of body language, emotional reactions and intuition. The second 'amber reflection' element looks at ethics, context, emotions and communication. The third 'green EQ application' element integrates the approach to emotional intelligence practice in communication with others and concludes with an emotionally intelligent leadership overview. The **EQ4U** model is then mapped to leadership practice and its application to different levels of leadership practice.

●	STOP	The 'red' element incorporates two stages. First, acknowledging and understanding your own body language and the emotions you feel associated with these, then listening to and reflecting on your intuitive 'inner voice'. Secondly, being aware of and aiming to understand others by being aware of their body language and behaviours, anticipating their emotions within the situation and actively listening to anything they have to say.
○	REFLECT	The 'amber' element means reflecting on the underpinning ethical framework that guides you, the overall situation, the interplay between yours and others' emotions, and an appropriate and effective way to communicate a response.
●	ACTION	The 'green' element is about choosing and then using an appropriately communicated reflective response which uses a blend of intuition and value matching to deal with both your own and others' emotions.

While the traffic lights model is intended as a simple metaphor to emphasise thought before action, what's important to note is that the EQ process is frequently quite complex. Depending on the circumstances involved, rather than a 'stop, caution, action' approach being the end of the process, awareness, reflection and response are recurring elements. Strictly speaking therefore, a more complete model of the process involved is as follows:

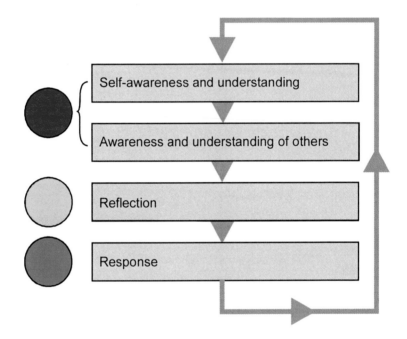

Self and Other Awareness and Understanding
(The 'red traffic light')

'It's what you learn after you know it all that counts.'
John Wooden
UCLA basket ball coach and author

It's important to understand ourselves before we can be effective in understanding others. The first (essential!) step however, before beginning the process of being more emotionally intelligent, is commitment. You have to be committed to developing your EQ and be willing to keep on trying to improve through the way you work and the things you do. Unlike making a commitment to learning a skill, personal development can be far more of a challenge because it addresses behaviour traits that may seem to be as ingrained as our personality and as difficult or even impossible to change. Assuming however that the desire and commitment to develop your EQ is in place, to help get you started, here are a few suggestions of activities you can undertake to get you moving in the right direction.

Self-awareness and understanding

There are 3 key aspects of self-awareness and understanding:

- being aware of and acknowledging own body language 'signals'
- understanding the emotions associated with these signs
- paying close attention to and reflecting on your intuitive feelings/gut reactions.

Within each of these aspects there are a number of components, with interrelationships and overlaps between them. The first stage of self-

167

awareness is instinctive; a complex combination of biological and cognitive forces with tendencies between them that may conflict or concur. (For further reading on this subject, see Professor Robert Winston's 'Human Instinct' - How our primeval impulses shape our modern lives', details in Part 4 – Learning Resources)

To develop self-awareness, think therefore about your emotional reactions to various events and ask yourself what causes these particular emotional reactions, at work or at home. To help you, here are a number of emotions that you may have felt at different times. Consider the emotions in Table 1 and ask yourself three questions:

1. When have I felt this particular emotion?
2. What caused it?
3. How did my emotional reaction affect how I acted?

Table 1: Emotions

Amused	Angry	Apprehensive	Ashamed
Brave	Calm	Comfortable	Confident
Depressed	Disgusted	Empathetic	Envious
Excited	Fearful	Friendly	Grief stricken
Guilty	Happy	Hopeful	Impatient
Jealous	Joyful	Remorseful	Repentant
Resentful	Resigned	Sad	Shocked
Surprised	Unhappy		

Self-awareness and body language

This initial self-awareness is often portrayed by our internal body language signals, such as tummy butterflies or sweaty palms when we are nervous, or subtle messages of calmness or concurrence portrayed for example, by relaxed shoulders or facial features. Learning to read the subliminal messages involved in our intuitive feelings allied with awareness and acknowledgement of our body language messages is a key tool of EQ development. Body language is however a complex phenomenon, whether it's ours or other people's. It involves a wide range of behaviours that communicate our feelings and emotions non-verbally both to ourselves as well as to others.

Further behaviours that indicate self-awareness are the body language signals we give to others that express our emotions. Paul Ekman, the world renowned expert on body language and emotion, suggests, *'We need to become more attentive to our emotions as we have them so there is a possibility of behaving emotionally in constructive ways'*. (See Paul Ekman's *'Emotions Revealed'* in Learning Resources) There is also an excellent source of information about the topic on the Internet, 'The Nonverbal Dictionary of Gestures, Signs & Body Language Cues' at:

http://members.aol.com/nonverbal2/diction1.htm

Before we propose a checklist of emotionally intelligent body language, reflecting on how you use your body when you are communicating to different people could be a useful starting point. Ask yourself how your body language differs in the various ways noted in Table 2, and what you think this means about your relationships with and feelings towards others, or about what is being said in your discussions with them:

Table 2: Body language

1. Body posture:
   a. Facing people, or turning away from them at an angle?
   b. Very upright and formal, or relaxed?
   c. Sitting or standing? What position are arms and legs in?
2. Proximity:
   a. Standing or sitting close to others?
   b. Touching people, and how (shaking hands, for example)?
3. Eye contact:
   a. Maintaining eye contact or looking away?
   b. Focusing on the person or at something around them?
4. Facial expression (Does this indicate the thoughts behind it?):
   a. Smiling at people, and how genuine this is? (Is it a 'smile with the

169

eyes' rather than just with the lips?)
b. Nodding or shaking the head when listening to others?
c. Raising eyebrows or making other facial signs?

While most of us are intuitively aware of our body language and the subliminal messages this may be giving to others, Table 3 is a useful checklist of emotionally intelligent non-verbal communication.

Table 3: EQ body language

1. Focusing on the individual/group involved, rather than being distracted by things around them.
2. Maintaining appropriate proximity by sitting or standing close enough to demonstrate interest, whilst being far enough away not to invade their 'personal space'.
3. Using 'open' hand movements, which indicate genuineness in what you are expressing (and also invites others to speak).
4. Standing or sitting in an upright but relaxed body position, rather than being stiff and formal or slouching.
5. Using body posture to face people, rather than turning away from them at an angle.
6. Greeting, and leaving, by shaking hands or using an appropriate body language greeting to reflect the relationship you have with them.
7. Using facial expressions that show interest and respect such as:
   a. Smiling genuinely, with your eyes as well as your mouth.
   b. Maintaining appropriate eye contact, rather than staring or avoiding eye contact.
   c. Using other facial signals that indicate you are listening.

By understanding how you use body language to signal your feelings, you will get a better insight into both what you are feeling, and how you are communicating those feelings to other people.

It is however important to emphasise that developing EQ is about learning to adapt both our emotional responses and our subsequent behaviour. A classic example portrayed in Robert Winston's television series 'The Human Mind' (BBC 1 – Summer 2004), was the driver whose automatic tendency was to get angry and aggressive whenever he came across other drivers he thought were incompetent. While it was acknowledged in the programme that ingrained traits can be difficult to change, it was also demonstrated that it is possible to achieve behaviour adjustments (or even a transformation!), by first of all having the will to succeed, and then by striving to develop different feelings. Aristotle's quote springs to mind:

'Anyone can become angry – that is easy. But to become angry with the right person, to the right degree, at the right time, for the right purpose and in the right way – that is not easy.'

Despite our inability to control what happens to us in a whole range of circumstances, we have the option to choose how we feel about the situations we find ourselves in and how to deal with them. An inspiring book that deals with the subject of destructive emotions and how we can overcome them, based on a dialogue with the Dalai Lama and narrated by Daniel Goleman, reflects on this subject in depth. (Further details in Learning Resources section) The book addresses questions about the root causes of destructive behaviours and how we can control the emotions driving these. The inspiring story of Victor Frankl and how he dealt with suffering and degradation while incarcerated in a Nazi prison camp during World War II is testament to this ability. The following are just two websites with information that may be of interest, including reference to his first book *'Man's Search for Meaning'*, written following his prison camp experiences:

http://www.selfhelpnetwork.com/Pages/SpiritualityInspiration.html

http://www.hypnos.co.uk/hypnomag/pdurbin4.htm

There's also an added benefit in choosing positive rather than negative feelings in health terms. Growing evidence of the link between psychological and physical health, and the consequent ability we have to influence our immune system and therefore our health by positive thought, is aptly described in *'Mind-Body Medicine'*, edited by Dr Alan Watson. (Further information in Learning Resources)

As part of our self-awareness, we can also choose to think assertively. This means having self-respect, having respect for others and being open and honest with both self and others. At the self-awareness stage, it means thinking positively, having high self-esteem, and believing that your needs, wants, feelings, rights and beliefs deserve the respect of others and should be balanced with theirs. As Eleanor Roosevelt put it so succinctly, *'No one can make you feel inferior without your consent'*. The initial thinking stage of being emotionally intelligent therefore includes underpinning thoughts of inner confidence based on self-respect and self-esteem.

To summarise, a 'self-awareness and understanding' approach means:

● developing a more conscious awareness of internal body language signals and what these might mean

● listening more closely to intuitive feelings that may have no conscious reasoning

● striving to adapt 'positive' rather than 'negative' emotional responses, guided by integrity based principles and values

● reflecting on emotional responses to situations and whether these are rational or appropriate and perhaps based on pre-judgement or prejudice; or whether they could be self managed to more productive alternatives

● self-affirmation by talking to yourself positively - for instance, *'I'm open to learn and I can change'* rather than *'I'm set in my ways'*.

Awareness and understanding of others

'Communication depends on our ability to make sense of the world as we perceive it and to understand the perceived world as others describe it.'

Geoff Cox
Artist, teacher, author, and lecturer in culture and technology at
Plymouth University

Understanding others, and the values, beliefs, motivators and other factors that influence their behaviour is an obvious attribute when seeking to build and maintain more effective relationships with either individuals or groups. Consciously recognising what emotion a person is feeling is emphasised by Paul Ekman in *'Emotions Revealed'* as a big step in improving communication. (Further details in Learning Resources section) If you want to become more emotionally intelligent, having a genuine interest in understanding others is essential. Showing empathy and connecting with others by being prepared to share your feelings and vulnerabilities and investing time and effort in building and maintaining trusted relationships also pays dividends if you want to become a more emotionally intelligent leader.

There are three key aspects of other awareness, i.e.:

● being interested in and aware of others' body language and behaviour
● encouraging them to say what they think and feel, and actively listening to what they have to say
● interpreting and anticipating their emotions (either individually or collectively) within the context of the situation.

As with self-awareness, within these elements there are a number of components, with interrelationships and overlaps between them. To develop other awareness, we also need to consider what others' emotional responses might include, such as those you looked at when considering emotions you may have felt and how they affected you. Consider the list in Table 1: Emotions, on page 168, and reflect on how others' emotional reactions may affect their behaviour as well as yours.

Paying attention to other people you work with, and asking yourself what emotions you think they may be portraying is part of being emotionally intelligent. Observing the signs people show of these different emotions and asking yourself what aspects of your behaviour could have influenced these emotions adds to your other awareness. In the case of negative emotions, like anger or sorrow, asking yourself what you could do to improve their emotional state indicates not only a level of emotional intelligence, but also empathy and consideration towards a fellow human being.

Other awareness and body language

Awareness of others' body language provides clues to help identify what emotions they may be feeling. Learning to read the subliminal body language messages others give to us (as well as the more obvious ones!) is especially helpful in trying to understand the emotions that may be involved. (These more subtle body language indicators are described by Paul Ekman as 'micro expressions'.) Awareness of others' body language and behaviour could include observation of the body language in Table 2 on page 169, followed by reflection on what you think this means about the person's relationship with you and feelings towards you.

You can use this list to review how effective you are at reading and making sense of other people's body language and see how your own behaviour and communication affects them. To produce more positive effects on people and help to build effective relationships through 'other awareness' body language, Table 3 on page 170, is a useful checklist of emotionally intelligent non-verbal communication.

To summarise, an 'other awareness and understanding' approach means:

- developing a more conscious awareness of others' body language signals and what these might mean
- anticipating others' likely emotional responses within the situation as you know it
- listening more closely to intuitive messages/inner feelings that you may have about others
- using body language towards others that shows respect and interest
- demonstrating empathy to others by showing a genuine interest in their concerns, beliefs etc., what they have to say and in actively listening to them
- connecting with others by being prepared to share your feelings and vulnerabilities
- investing time and effort in building and maintaining productive relationships and developing mutual trust.

Reflection
(The 'amber traffic light')

Reflection can be described as an internal process giving serious thought or consideration as a precursor to action. This may relate to your intuitive feelings, concerns, issues and circumstances and/or the concerns, issues and circumstances of others. It means mentally looking back on experience, knowledge and learning in order to come to a decision about how to deal with these, before expressing yourself in either words or deeds.

Reflection is essential to being emotionally intelligent, and fundamental to developing emotional competence. The emphasis is therefore on thought before action, and considered responses rather than instant gut reactions (that you may well later regret!).

There are four key aspects to **EQ4U** reflection. It means giving serious thought or consideration to:

* your ethical framework of principles and values
* the overall situation, including own and others' circumstances
* your own emotions and others' anticipated emotions
* the appropriate way to communicate your response.

1. Your ethical framework

What is the basis for your ethical system? How much thought do you normally give to questions about what you believe in and how you judge core issues about right and wrong?

Try asking yourself the following questions to help you get some insight into your ethical system and the principles and values that guide you:

* What do you believe are the most important principles or values that shape (or should shape) your behaviour at work?

* Do you believe that these are generally shared by others you work

176

with, or are there some who hold different opinions about what is the right and proper thing to do?

- Have you ever been faced with a situation in which you felt pressured to do something that you believed was wrong? How did you react? In retrospect, do you believe you did the right thing?

- Have you seen other people you know faced with a situation in which they were pressured to do something that you believed was wrong? How did you react? In retrospect, do you believe you did the right thing?

- Do you believe that there are circumstances where it would be appropriate to do something wrong in order to produce an outcome that was morally right, or do you believe that the end can never justify the means? In other words, do you believe that you should always do the morally right thing even if it were to produce an outcome that may be unpleasant, uncomfortable, or has even more significant consequences?

- In either case, have you been faced with a situation where you had to make a decision where there was conflict between the ends and the means (i.e. do the wrong thing to produce a beneficial outcome, or do the right thing even though the outcome would be unwelcome)? What did you do? Do you believe, in retrospect, that it was the correct decision to make?

- Thinking about your answers to these questions, do you feel that you always strive to live up to the most important principles and values that you believe in? Is there anything that you could or should do to exhibit your principles and values more clearly, in your decisions or your behaviour?

2. The overall situation

It's important to be aware of and understand as far as possible, the context within which interactions with others take place. The danger otherwise, is that incorrect assumptions may be made that influence your approach in dealing with these, which may well result in decisions being made that have damaging consequences. It's helpful therefore to understand the background that forms the setting of an event and to ask yourself the following:

- How well do you take full account of the circumstances affecting decisions that you are faced with?
- Do you actively ask questions and seek other people's views before making decisions; and genuinely listen and take note of their responses?
- Do you ask people how they feel about possible options (their emotional response), as well as what information they have (their knowledge and understanding)?
- What could you do to consider these issues more in making decisions and generally interacting with others?

3. Your own and others' anticipated emotions

Reflecting on both your own emotions and anticipating what others' emotions may be, is inherent to the **EQ4U** process. Thinking about some decisions you have made recently or tasks that you have performed:

- Did you reflect on how you felt about issues as well as what you thought about them?
- When you were making the decisions or undertaking the tasks, did you feel at all uneasy about what you were doing? Did these feelings cause you to review or even change what you did?
- On the other hand, did you ever tend to go with your feelings, come what may? How well did you reflect on your feelings in the light of your knowledge about the situation and manage the way that you allowed your emotions to shape your behaviour?
- What about the emotional reactions of others, how they felt about the situation? To what extent did you consider these and allow them to shape your behaviour?
- Alternatively, did you tend to make other people's feelings the

guiding principle in your behaviour? In retrospect, was this the best way to behave?

4. Communication

Thinking about your communication skills and how effective they are in four key aspects helps to convey your message in an emotionally intelligent way. The most effective communicators:

a) demonstrate that they understand the situation
b) are clear, concise and logical in their presentation
c) convey openness and honesty
d) show an appropriate degree of warmth depending on the relationship/s and circumstances.

Reflecting on a match with these four aspects helps to convey a clear, appropriate and genuine message, whatever communication method you use.

Thinking about some recent events where you have communicated with others, it's useful to ask yourself the following questions:

● In what way did my communication show that I recognised and understood the context?
● Was the message clear and appropriate?
● Did people react as if they believed I was being genuine, open and honest?
● Did I demonstrate an appropriate degree of warmth?

Reflection is a complex and essentially personal process. Going through the steps of conscious and focused reflection on your ethical framework of principles and values, the context of each situation (including your own and others' circumstances), your own and others' emotions helps to formulate what might be an appropriate way to communicate a response.

To summarise, an emotionally intelligent reflective process means:

- having a clear framework of principles and values to guide your behaviour
- recognising your own and others' emotions within the overall context
- planning an effectively communicated response that demonstrates your understanding of the situation, that is clear, concise and genuine - and conveys openness, honesty and an appropriate degree of warmth.

EQ – Application
(The 'green traffic light')

Applied EQ means communicating with others in a way that recognises yours and others' emotions, underpinned by a framework of ethical principles and values. While there may be many difficult or challenging decisions that need to be made, if serious thought and reflection has gone into these beforehand, then the action that you choose to take is likely to be more straightforward.

There are three aspects to **EQ4U** application. It means responding with behaviour that reflects:

1. recognition of own and others' emotions
2. a match with ethical principles and values
3. an appropriate communication protocol.

Think about situations that you have recently been in where you have had to make critical decisions or undertake critical tasks.

- Did you take account of your own emotions when deciding what to do?
- Did you behave in ways that showed that you recognised others' emotions?

Again, thinking about those same situations:

- Did your behaviour match your own ethical principles and values?
- Did you communicate effectively with the others affected so that they understood what you were doing, why you were doing it and that you understood how they would be likely to feel about your behaviour?

While these EQ leadership practices relate to managers at every level, different levels of management have particular responsibilities in the

181

way that they use their power and authority. For senior managers, it means using power and authority within an ethical framework in establishing purpose, vision and values, formulating objectives, setting strategy and structure, defining policies and in taking any decisions critical to organisational performance. For operational managers, it means using power and authority in a fair and equitable manner in delegating to others, defining procedures and monitoring performance; and for team leaders, it means maximising productivity through fair and equitable supervisory practice.

The following checklist summarises the **EQ4U** approach and behaviours within the four stages and three elements involved, and is designed to help you learn about yourself and your own behaviour in a range of circumstances as a leader and manager. Using it regularly will help you to review your approach and the development of your EQ. There is no point of perfection where you have achieved a faultless score. Instead, there is only the possibility of improving yourself and raising your EQ. It doesn't happen overnight, but is a slow and gradual process. However, it starts the moment you work through the checklist, because it means that you are raising your awareness and developing your reflective abilities.

To lead with integrity-based emotional intelligence:

- develop more conscious self-awareness and understanding through listening attentively to intuitive feelings, reflecting on emotional responses to leadership situations and whether they could be self managed to more productive alternatives

- have a clear framework of principles and values to guide your behaviour, and maintain beliefs, commitment and effort in spite of setbacks or opposition

- understand and resist personal pressures which encourage non-ethical behaviour and work towards the resolution of ethical dilemmas

---

- be tuned in to your body language and its impact on others; confirm others' understanding through questioning and interpretation of both verbal responses and non-verbal signals

- develop a more conscious awareness of others' body language signals, the emotions they may be feeling and an appropriate way to deal with these

- demonstrate empathy to others by showing a genuine interest in their concerns, beliefs and priorities

- remain calm in difficult or uncertain situations, act in an assured and unhesitating manner when faced with a challenge and stand up for your legitimate rights in a way that does not violate the rights of others

- stand up for others' rights in a way that matches your principles and values while acknowledging both your own and others' emotions within the overall context of the circumstances involved

- make constructive efforts to resolve any disagreements

- communicate to others in a clear, concise and genuine way that demonstrates an understanding of context, and convey your message with an appropriate degree of warmth

- adopt communication styles appropriate to listeners and situations, selecting a relevant time and place and speaking clearly with a steady tone, standard pitch and even pace

- distinguish clearly between fact and opinion, focusing on facts, problems and solutions when handling an emotional situation

- invest time and effort in building and maintaining productive relationships and in developing mutual trust

- connect with others and genuinely try to understand them by listening attentively, and by being prepared to share your feelings and vulnerabilities

- regularly review and evaluate your leadership and management performance and the outcomes resulting from your decisions and actions; be open and honest in evaluating your own strengths and weaknesses

- actively seek feedback about your behaviour and performance, noting this non-defensively, acknowledge when you have made a mistake and apologise when this is appropriate.

- change behaviour where needed and be receptive to continual learning and change; i.e., be open to 'mind change' rather than 'mindset'.

Process mapping against the stages of **EQ4U** for senior managers, operational managers and team leaders is outlined in the following section. You may also find it useful to refer to the 'Relationship Investments' exercise for developing more productive relationships with others through emotional intelligence, available via the **EQ4U** website noted in Part 4 – Learning Resources.

How does the MINDCHANGE EQ4U process model apply to senior managers?

The **MINDCHANGE EQ4U PROCESS** is designed to be used to help explain behaviour and to help determine what behaviour may be appropriate in the circumstances. **EQ4U** can also be used here to understand the principles that guide the behaviour of senior managers to enable them to develop their emotional competence.

Self-awareness and understanding

Senior managers can have feelings – it is allowed! Many of the decisions that they have to make are so significant that they have the potential to affect the whole future of the organisation and the careers and future lives of their employees. This is frightening stuff and senior managers should be prepared to acknowledge the fear – feel it and deal with it, and in the right circumstances, be prepared to share their principles and values and what they passionately believe in as a leader. The alternative is to present an unfeeling or ruthless image that may suit some and conform to an out of date model of leadership, but it doesn't convince those affected by the decisions. Instead, it creates the image of an unfeeling and uncaring person, one who may manage but does not lead.

Awareness and understanding of others

Senior managers often feel remote from those they lead, a remoteness caused by the length of the communication channels they use and by the nature of their role. Remoteness is sometimes welcomed by senior managers, as a way of emphasising their positional power, with the mistaken belief that the further they are from the people they lead, the greater their power must be. By being inaccessible and distancing themselves from people, senior managers are however unable to authentically gauge the effect of their decisions on the people involved. A lack of awareness and understanding of how people feel also means they are unlikely to know how their decisions will be implemented, such as those relating to organisational policies and direction.

Reflection

The lessons of Enron, WorldCom and the many other organisations that crashed in the late nineties were simple – their senior management had deluded themselves that the ethical principles that governed others didn't govern them. They had somehow transcended the everyday world of right and wrong and were now in the world of increasing financial returns where the rightness of an action was measured by the profit and loss account. The result was that once they started lying to others, they were able to lie to themselves, to delude themselves about the reality of the situation they were in. They could no longer distinguish what is, from what they wanted it to be, and built up organisations that were ultimately weak and that failed on a scale that had previously been unimagined.

Being ethical and honest starts with yourself, being true to your own beliefs and values so that you can carry others with you. This leads, in turn, to getting a better understanding of the situation you find yourself in, and how others will react (as opposed to how you want them to). Finally, you don't have to worry about what you told them last time if you told them the truth. Once you start misleading others, you finish up misleading yourself.

EQ – Application

If all this sounds high-minded, it isn't, it's immensely practical. Being honest is not the same as revealing all – there are always limits on what you can say and do, limits based on the need for confidentiality and often simply because people don't have to know everything, or they would otherwise be overloaded. Senior managers set the tone for their organisations, and their behaviour will influence everyone. The role of the emotionally intelligent leader is to set direction and establish the principles by which the organisation will operate, and to do this by demonstration and not by edict. It means using your influence as a leader to ensure that the organisation's policies and practices take due note of their impact on people, and applying the power of both words and actions to inspire others towards achievement. Leadership is about creating followers, and people will follow the leaders they trust and they believe in, wherever they may lead them.

How does the MINDCHANGE EQ4U process model apply to operational managers?

The **MINDCHANGE EQ4U PROCESS** model can also be used here to understand the principles that guide the behaviour of operational managers to enable them to develop their emotional competence.

Self-awareness and understanding

For this group of managers, their feelings often relate to individuals and groups both above and below them in the hierarchy. The way they react to what their managers say, or what is said to them by those they manage, will be filtered thought their own emotional relationships and reactions. And, because they are often in regular contact with the people they manage, they are constantly sending out signals to them by the way they behave and how they appear. A whole office or production unit can take its cue from the emotional state of the line manager who walks through it in the morning. Along with managers at all levels, operational managers need to be aware of their own feelings if they are to govern their impact on others.

Awareness and understanding of others

Because this group of managers is directly responsible for the actions of others, they need to be alert to how people are responding to them and to each other. Internal rivalries and tensions can seriously undermine the effectiveness of any work group and individuals' personal problems can seriously affect their performance. Managers need to recognise how others are reacting to their environment and to each other, and be prepared to take action in response to this.

Reflection

Managers at this level need to be able to speak the language of 'things' - to be effective, they need a deep understanding of the people and operations they are managing – and to do so with consistency and openness. Any discrepancies in what they say or do will be picked up and broadcast, because people being social animals, they constantly monitor the behaviour of others. Consistency in words and deeds is so much easier if action is guided by a coherent set of values and principles. Know what you believe in and what the organisation's values and principles are, be alert to any conflicts and work out how you can resolve them. Any significant dissonance between the two can otherwise cause long term problems.

EQ – Application

By being honest to yourself you will be honest to others. By operating consistently in relation to your principles and values you will demonstrate consistency to others and encourage them to share and commit those same values and principles. By showing through your behaviour what you believe in and what is important, whilst acknowledging and understanding the feelings of the people you manage, you will maintain their respect and build effective relationships with them.

How does the MINDCHANGE EQ4U process model apply to team leaders?

The **MINDCHANGE EQ4U PROCESS** model can also be used here to understand the principles that guide the behaviour of team leaders to enable them to develop their emotional competence.

Self awareness and understanding

Team Leaders at a supervisory level, can often feel highly vulnerable in their role, being accountable for themselves and others, invariably without much in the way of management authority to match. They often feel uncertain as to where they stand – with responsibilities limited to those at an overseeing level, but at the same time they are not the same as other members of the team. They can often find themselves doing the jobs that others don't want on the basis that they can't ask them to do it if they don't do it themselves. All this can make being a team leader's role ambiguous and therefore difficult, with a need to recognise this ambiguity and the difficult position they often find themselves in, especially when they find themselves with split loyalties between the managers they are accountable to and the team they are part of (as well as lead).

Awareness and acknowledgement of this is the first step to reconciling these competing pressures. Too many team leaders try to avoid the problem by not accepting the responsibilities of the management aspects of the role, and try to remain one of the team. This simply avoids the problem, rather than resolving it. By understanding the issues involved and the dichotomy of the role, team leaders can then start rising to meet the challenge.

Awareness and understanding of others

Because of their closeness to the team, team leaders are likely to have the best insights into how others feel. Using this understanding of the people in their team helps them to recognise their different personalities and attributes and how this affects both team and individual performance. Focusing closely on how people are likely to react within a given situation and preparing for the results enables them to lead people through this rather than force them.

Reflection

The difficulty that team leaders experience, of having a foot in both the management and the team camps presents real pressures. The resolution is to be clear about what really matters to them and use this to guide their response to any situation, especially when dealing with what may often seem conflicting loyalties. Focused reflection on what they feel and believe, and what others are likely to feel and believe is a key part of the process; notably in understanding why decisions further up the management hierarchy are being made and what the potential impact might be on the people they lead. Reflecting on the best way to communicate the impact of these decisions and what is needed clearly and honestly to their team is the best way forward.

EQ – Application

As with middle and first line managers, team leaders need to be consistent in what they do and how they do it, what they say and how they say it. Given their closeness to the people they lead, every action will be under scrutiny and so team leaders probably have more need to focus on their application than anybody else. By being true to themselves, this becomes so much easier than by trying to live up to an artificial model of what they think should be done.

'It is a terrible thing to look over your shoulder when you are trying to lead – and find no one there.'
Franklin D. Roosevelt

Closing Reflections

2004, the year that we wrote the main body of **MINDCHANGE** was dominated by news from the Iraq war, and concluded with the tragedy of the Asian Tsunami. The one exposed deep divisions within and between countries around the world, the other brought people together as never before. In both cases emotions were dominant in people's reactions. However, the most intense reminder of the impact of emotions prior to the publication of **MINDCHANGE** was the 60th anniversary of the liberation of Auschwitz on 27th January 2005. Despite the length of time involved, the scale and the depth of suffering endured by those who survived the atrocities perpetrated by the Nazi regime at Auschwitz and in other death camps left both intense and long-lasting emotional scars that remain to this day.

A lack of emotionally intelligent leadership can have repercussions that go way beyond the individuals and groups directly involved. As human beings with human failings, we are guilty of not always showing due consideration and respect for others' values, beliefs and circumstances, and the emotions relating to these. Allied with limited recognition and understanding of our own feelings and how to deal with these with integrity, the results of interactions where both parties' emotions have not been taken into account can range from damaged relationships to extremes of psychological and/or physical mistreatment.

We make no excuse, therefore, for concluding with reference to an emotionally charged military event, because a single incident revealed how easy it is when people are not properly led or managed, for their behaviour to fall far short of the standards we all expect. This incident is the widely reported torture and humiliation of Iraqi prisoners at Abu Graib, in 2004. The emotional damage experienced by the victims can only be imagined, but the negative repercussions reverberate not only amongst the people and the organisations involved, but also impact on the wider global community. As Tahseen Hassan the husband of Margaret Hassan commented when trying to come to terms with her abduction in Bagdad on 19th October 2004 (and subsequent murder), *'What is a human being but a bundle of emotional nerves?'*

The need for listening and understanding is emphasised by Alex Bomberg of International Intelligence, whose experience of working within Iraq as well as in other conflict situations, drew the conclusion that *'We need to be thinking about hearts and minds, not bullets and guns'*. As Napoleon Bonaparte noted, *'Even in war, moral power is to physical as three parts out of four'*.

Our concluding messages of **MINDCHANGE** are these:

● **Management and leadership are integrated and essential abilities requiring a blend of intellectual ability and emotional intelligence.**

● **Leaders, both individually and collectively, have significant power and responsibility to influence positive change and benefit business productivity, social and political outcomes through emotionally intelligent 'contagion'.**

● **Developing EQ is no 'quick fix', but an ongoing process of learning and reflective practice; building and maintaining trust and valued relationships are essential elements.**

MINDCHANGE challenges leaders in whatever environment they lead and at whatever level they function, to strive continuously to be more emotionally aware of self and others, and through reflective practice deal with the pressures of the leadership decisions they face with emotional competence. Emotionally competent leadership is therefore not about 'transformational' or 'heroic' leadership, but is more an ability to recognise and to tune into others' feelings, to inspire and to energise towards a shared commitment. Otherwise the danger that we face at local, national and international levels is a downward spiral of distrust which harms organisations and people. The power of emotionally intelligent leadership is shaping destiny and winning strategy through recognition and understanding of own and others' emotions, and using integrity and intuition to guide behaviour.

Resources

'But words are things, and a small drop of ink,
Falling like dew, upon a thought, produces,
That which makes thousands, perhaps millions, think'
Lord Byron

Learning Resources for EQ leadership and teams includes a list of books, websites and other items referred to throughout MINDCHANGE. These are listed in page order and are either specifically about emotional intelligence or those that we believe make an effective contribution to personal development and leadership effectiveness.

Further information, including books, articles and handouts, web links and interactive resources, can be found on the EQ4U Learning Resources website **www.eq4u.co.uk**. The books listed on this site include some of our favourite personally recommended texts that may be of interest to readers, which have not been noted within **MINDCHANGE** itself. We regularly update our list on this site and would be delighted to hear from you if you have any comments or recommendations.

Jan Childs

Email: jan.childs@mdplimited.co.uk

David Pardey

Email: david@teamsthatwork.co.uk

Page 14 – Daniel Goleman, *'Working with Emotional Intelligence'* (1998) Work done at the University of Wisconsin's Laboratory for Affective Neuroscience has shown that women respond both physiologically and psychologically quite differently to their own children compared to other children. A movie showing data from a functional magnetic resonance imaging (fMRI) brain scan, which can be downloaded from their website (**http://www.news.wisc.edu/packages/emotion/media.html**) illustrates this quite clearly. One area of the brain activates when mothers see their own infants; another area activates when they see someone else's child.

Page 18 – Paul Ekman the world renowned psychologist and expert on non-verbal communication shares insights of his experience and findings of 40 years research in *'Emotions Revealed: Understanding Faces and Feelings'* (Weidenfeld & Nicolson: 2003). The practical lessons shared in the book help in particular with self and other awareness and understanding (the first two steps of the **MINDCHANGE EQ4U PROCESS**), and shows how we can apply this learning to both leadership and personal circumstances.

Page 18 – The online encyclopaedia, Wikipedia, (**http://en.wikipedia.org/ wiki/Emotions**) is major, truly open source web encyclopaedia that is created by its users. Not only is its breadth of coverage amazing, but it exists because those who submit articles do so primarily to benefit the rest of the world's Internet users.

Page 20 – Simon Baron-Cohen, a Cambridge Professor and co-director of the Autism Research Centre there, describes empathy in his book The Essential Difference (Allen Lane: 2003). Baron-Cohen's questionnaire, included in his book and also available on-line at: **http://www.guardian.co.uk/life/flash/page/0,13249,937836,00.html**

Page 24 – Thinking complexity often leads to confusion. The '6 Hats' method of thinking simplifies the process by dealing with emotion, logic, hope, information and creativity separately and within a coherent framework. Edward de Bono's best selling *Six Thinking Hats* (Penguin Books: 1999) outlines how to make best use of everyone's intelligence, experience and information by using this approach.

Page 27 – Costa and McCrae's "OCEAN model" of personality consists of Openness, Conscientiousness, Extraversion, Agreeableness and Neuroticism – there is more detail about it at and links to an open source personality test at:
http://forbin.mit.edu/RiskAndPreferences/personalitymodels.jsp

Page 32 – Mayer and Salovey *'Emotional intelligence'* in *Imagination, Cognition and Personality* volume 9. Their Four Branch Model of Emotional Intelligence is explained in detail in their various books and on Mayer's website – see below for details:
http://baywood.com/journals/default.asp

Page 36 – Robert K. Cooper & Ayman Sawaf *'Executive EQ: Emotional Intelligence in Business'* (Orion Business: 1997). This book shares insights into the value and application of emotional intelligence in achieving commercial as well as personal benefits, and is of special interest to those who operate at a senior level of management. It includes both a range of case studies highlighting the application (or otherwise) of EQ and an 'EQ map' for self assessment. The case studies included provide additional and valuable learning points to those we have covered in **MINDCHANGE**, and the emphasis on the benefits of EQ application to strategic leadership.

Page 37 – Anabel Jensen (with Joshua Freedman *'Handle With Care'* (Six Seconds: 2001); Esther Orioli *'EQ Map'* (Essi Systems: 1997), Geetu Orme (formerly Bharwaney) *'Emotionally Intelligent Living'* (Crown House Publishing: 2001) and David Caruso (with Peter Salovey) *'The Emotionally Intelligent Manager'* (Jossey Bass)

Page 39 - *'Key Readings on the Mayer and Salovey Model'*, edited by Salovey, Brackett and Mayer (National Professional Resources Inc: 2004 – http://www.NPRinc.com)

Page 83 – Joseph Boyett and Jimmie Boyett *'The Guru Guide – the best ideas of the top management thinkers'* (John Wiley & Sons 2000)

Page 45 – *Psychological Review* (**http://www.apa.org/journals/rev.html**)

Page 52 – Mark McCormack *'What they don't teach you at Harvard Business School'* (Profile Business: 1994)

Page 59 – Peter Fusaro and Ross Miller *'What went wrong at Enron'* (John Wiley & Sons: 2002) reveals how easy it is for an organisation to go badly wrong when leaders forget their purpose.

Page 61 – Keith Brody and Sancha Dunstan *'The Great Telecoms Swindle'* (Capstone Publishing Ltd: 2003) reveals the many delusions brought about by the explosion of telecoms-related businesses in the 1990s.

Page 62 – John Plender *'Going off the Rails'* (John Wiley and Sons: 2003) shows how an emotional commitment to the benefits of market capitalism can blind people to the problems it produces.

Page 63 – Max Bazerman, George Loewenstein and Don Moore Harvard *Business Review* ('Why Good Accountants Do Bad Audits' HBR Nov. 2002 pp. 97-102)

Page 68 – Dr Carsten Sørensen of the London School of Economics and Political Science, commissioned by Microsoft and entitled *'The Future Role of Trust in Work'* is available from: **http://www.microsoft.com/uk/business/trustinwork/default.mspx**

Page 68 – IABC Research Foundation for United Technologies *'Measuring Organisational Trust: A Diagnostic Survey and International Indicator'* is available from: **http://store.yahoo.com/iabcstore/measortrus.html**)

Page 79 - *'The Change Masters'* Rosabeth Moss Kanter (Unwin Hynam 1985). Kanter is a specialist in the development and implementation of corporate strategy, but within her exploration of what makes for successful strategic management she underscores the message that is at the heart of MINDCHANGE – that it is the relationship between individuals and the extent to which the organisation creates a climate within which people can work together to achieve a clearly articulated vision that makes the difference between success and failure.

Page 80 – Chuck Palus and David Horth *'The Leader's Edge'* (Center for Creative Leadership: 2002). We have quoted Chuck Paulus in **MINDCHANGE** because of the emphasis he and David Horth (and the Centre for Creative Leadership where they work) place on the importance of creativity in organisational success, and on the centrality of effective leadership for encouraging that creativity. At the centre of this leadership is the ability to understand yourself and your own passions (what makes you want to commit to ideas and behaviours) and to work with others. Along with other researchers, they have concluded that it is the skills of self-awareness and awareness of others that lie at the heart of creative leadership.

Page 87 – Lawrence Appley *'Formula for success: A core concept of management'* (AMACOM: 1974). We have used Lawrence Appley's definition of management ('Getting things done through other people') in **MINDCHANGE** because it says so simply what many other definitions struggle to say. But there is more to Appley than this, and in this seminal book he lays down four basic principles of management that are also recognisably relevant to our beliefs. They are that managers (and leaders) should be:

- responsive to an orderly approach (stop and think – the red light)
- dependent upon unique skills and tools (and **MINDCHANGE** has been all about developing some of these skills)
- guided by a code of ethics
- controlled by disciplines.

It is too easy to think that all we know about management and leadership has been discovered in the last few years. Appley shows that many of today's ideas have been around for years and that the challenge is to put them into practice.

Page 90 – Richard Boyatzis co-wrote *Primal Leadership* with Daniel Goleman and Annie McKee (Harvard Business School Press: 2002)

Page 93 – Colin Powell & Joseph Persico *'A Soldier's Way'* (Hutchinson: 1996)

Page 93 – Rensis Likert *'The Human Organization: Its Management and Value'* (McGraw-Hill: 1967) - one of the seminal books on leadership and management.

Page 94 – Robert Blake and Jane Moulton *'The Managerial Grid'* (Gulf Publishing Company: 1978)

Page 94 – Paul Hersey and Kenneth Blanchard *'Management of organizational behaviour'* (Prentice-Hall: 1982)

Page 168 - *'Human Instinct'* by Robert Winston (Bantam Press 2002). In "Human Instinct", which accompanied a BBC1 television series, Robert Winston looks at the role of human instinct in shaping our behaviour and how this relates to the way we live. While this book is not directly related to the development of emotional intelligence, it provides a useful insight into how our instincts and emotions relate to each other and how this knowledge can help towards a better understanding of both ourselves and others.

Page 171 - *'Destructive Emotions – and how we can overcome them'*, A dialogue by the Dalai Lama narrated by Daniel Goleman (Bloomsbury Publishing Plc, London 2003). Buddhist wisdom, neuroscience and psychology integrate to provide valuable insights into how we can recognise and transform the interpersonal conflicts that result in destructive emotions that have the potential to harm us both individually and collectively. **MINDCHANGE** emphasises the reflective process and the capacity we have to change our emotions and thus our approach to dealing with situations. This book presents a valuable read to those interested in in-depth study of how to achieve this.

Page 98 – John P. Kotter *'Leading Change'* (McGraw-Hill: 1996)

Page 98 – James Kouzes and Barry Posner *'The Leadership Challenge'* (Jossey Bass 3rd edition 2003) They argue that effective leadership is based upon a few, really important, behaviours. This best-selling book emphasises the importance of vision and values, of behaving in ways that reflect those values, and of engaging people's hearts and not just their minds. Once again, where Kouzes and Posner lay down the principles of behaviour, **MINDCHANGE** provides the detailed guidance on how you should act to put them into practice, through development of your EQ.

Page 100 – Chris Pierce (ed.) *'The Effective Director: The Essential Guide to Director and Board Development'* (Kogan Page 2001). A useful guide to both established and newly appointed company directors on their role and responsibilities on the management board. The book includes an emphasis on the need for influencing and leading strategic direction. It provides helpful insights and practical guidance to senior managers in their role both as a leader and a member of a management team.

Index